MEXICO

MEXICO

SECOND EDITION

Michael D. Coe
Yale University

PRAEGER PUBLISHERS
New York

Published by arrangement with Thames and Hudson, London
First published in 1962 in
the 'Ancient Peoples and Places' series
Second edition 1977
© 1962 and 1977 Michael D. Coe
All rights reserved.

Published in the United States of America in 1977
by Praeger Publishers
200 Park Avenue, New York, N.Y. 10017
A Division of Holt, Rinehart and Winston

Library of Congress Catalog Card Number: 75-36199

ISBN   0 – 03 – 038431 – 1 pbk.
ISBN   0 – 03 – 028526 – 7

Printed in the United States of America

7 8 9   090   9 8 7 6 5 4 3 2 1

CONTENTS

List of Illustrations

FIGURES

Foreword

The subject matter of this book is the story of the pre-Spanish peoples of Mexico, who with their neighbours the Maya were the most advanced of the American Indians. As it will be used here, the term *Mexico* will mean all of the land in that Republic which lies between the western border of the Maya and the northern frontier where Mexican farmers once met the nomadic tribesmen of the desert.

I have found it both feasible and justifiable to exclude the ancient Maya from this survey, although part of their territory was, in fact, within the boundaries of the present day *Estados Unidos de México*. The Maya civilisation of the Yucatan Peninsula and Central America was so extraordinarily complex that to do it justice would be impossible within the confines of the present volume. Those remarkable people would appear to have placidly remained within their own borders throughout the centuries, so that other American Indian cultures of the Republic can be considered quite independently without the problem of Maya influences seriously conflicting with the development of our theme. *The Maya*, the companion to this volume in the series, appeared in 1966 and should be read with it.

Some may be disappointed to find the Aztec empire confined to a single chapter. 'Aztec' and 'Mexico' seem almost synonymous, but we now know that in the total span of man's occupation of that country, the Aztecs were late arrivals, their empire but a final and brilliant flicker before the light of native civilisation was put out once and for all. I have used the simpler rendering *Moctezuma* for the third and seventh Aztec kings in place of the more correct *Motecuhzoma*; the familiar 'Montezuma' of numberless boyhood romances is hopelessly incorrect.

Another matter which must be touched upon is the pronunciation of the very formidable-looking words and names of ancient Mexico. The matter is relatively quite simple, since they were transcribed in Roman letters in terms of the language spoken by the *conquistadores* of the sixteenth century. Thus, vowels and most consonants are generally pronounced as they would be in modern Spanish, with these exceptions:

x has the sound of the English *sh*, as it once had in Spanish (witness the derivation of 'sherry' from the Spanish *Xerez*).

tl – in this cluster, the *l* is a voiceless surd consonant, much like the Welsh *ll*.

As in Spanish, *hu* before a vowel is to be pronounced like English *w*.

A great deal of archaeological water has gone over the dam since *Mexico* appeared in 1962. The most exciting new research includes the Tehuacán Project directed by Richard S. MacNeish, the quest for the roots of Olmec civilisation, and the photogrammetric mapping of the ancient New World's largest city by René Millon. These and other new findings are included in the present volume.

Many persons have very kindly aided me in the preparation of this book. I would like to mention especially Richard S. MacNeish, Paul C. Mangelsdorf, Edward Deevey, Paul Sears, Geoffrey H. S. Bushnell, and Roman Piña Chán for their generous help, as well as those listed in 'Sources of Illustrations'. My wife, Sophie D. Coe, read and provided useful criticism for all the chapters.

M.D.C.

Chronological Table

DATES	PERIODS	CENTRAL HIGHLANDS	NORTH AND CENTRAL GULF COAST PLAIN	SOUTHERN GULF COAST PLAIN	OAXACA	GRIJALVA DEPRESSION AND THE SOUTH-EAST
1520	LATE POST-CLASSIC	Aztec Empire			Mixtec states	Chiapa XII (Chiaptanec state)
1200		'Feudal' states				
	EARLY POST-CLASSIC	Tula and the Toltecs			Mitla ('Monte Albán IV')	Chiapa XI
900	LATE CLASSIC	Coyotlatelco	Classic El Tajín, Veracruz Remojadas		Monte Albán III–B	Chiapa X
600						Chiapa IX
	EARLY CLASSIC	Teotihuacán III		Cerro de la Mesas, Late Tres Zapotes	Monte Albán III–A	Chiapa VIII
300		Teotihuacán II			Monte Albán II	Chiapa VII
		Teotihuacán I				Chiapa VI
A.D.	LATE FORMATIVE	Chupícuaro				Izapa
B.C.		Cuicuilco		Early Tres Zapotes		Chiapa V
300					Monte Albán I	Chiapa IV
	MIDDLE FORMATIVE	Zacatenco		Olmec civilisation (La Venta)		Chiapa III
		El Arbolillo I				Chiapa II
1000	EARLY FORMATIVE	Tlatilco		Olmec civilisation (San Lorenzo)		Chiapa I (Cotorra)
1500	(ARCHAIC)					

12

CHAPTER I

Introduction

The ancient cultures of Mexico along with the Maya civilisation comprise the larger entity known to archaeologists as 'Mesoamerica', a name first proposed by Paul Kirchhoff and including much of the great constriction that separates the masses of North and South America. Above all, the peoples of Mesoamerica were farmers, and had been for thousands of years isolated from the simple cultivating societies of the American South-west and South-east by the desert wastes of northern Mexico, through which only semi-nomadic, hunting aborigines ranged in pre-Spanish times. Beyond the southern borders of Mesoamerica lay the petty chiefdoms of lower Central America, not distinguished by any achievements other than a high production of fine ceramics and quantities of gold ornaments, lavishly heaped in the tombs of their great.

Further south yet, in Ecuador, Peru, and Bolivia, was the Andean Area, most noted for its final glory, the immense Inca Empire, but having native civilisations as far back in time as the eighth century before Christ. The Andean Area and Mesoamerica were the twin peaks of American Indian cultural development, from which all else in the Western Hemisphere seems both peripheral and derived.

Setting them off from the rest of the New World, the diverse cultures of Mesoamerica shared in a number of features which were pretty much confined to their area. Among these are hieroglyphic writing; bark-paper or deer-skin books which fold like screens; maps; a complicated calendar based on the permutation of a 260-day 'year' with the solar year of 365 days; an extensive knowledge of astronomy; a team game resembling basketball played in a special court with a solid rubber ball; markets and favoured 'ports of trade'; wars for the purpose of securing sacrificial victims; large-scale human sacrifice; private confession and penance by self-mutilation; tobacco-smoking; and a pantheon of extraordinary complexity, but usually including a rain god and a culture hero who was known as the Feathered Serpent.

Naturally, the peoples of Mesoamerica followed a number of other customs which are rather widespread among New World Indians, but their typical method of food preparation as a unified complex appears to be unique. The basis of the diet was the triad of maize, beans, and squash. Maize was, and still is, prepared by soaking it overnight or boiling it with lime and grinding it with a hand stone (Spanish *mano*) on a trough- or saddle-shaped quern (*metate*, from the Náhuatl *metlatl*). The resulting dough is either toasted by the housewife as flat cakes known as *tortillas* or else steamed or boiled as *tamales*. Always and everywhere in Mesoamerica, the hearth is comprised of three stones and is semi-sacred.

How far back in time can this pattern be extended? Given our present information, Mesoamerica as a great unit of aboriginal American culture appears to be as old as the earliest appearance of farming societies – but, it should be considered inherently improbable that all of the traits of this entity appeared at once with the primary domestication of maize. Early cultures evolved incredibly slowly, not by the quantum leaps so apparent in the modern world.

THE GEOGRAPHIC SETTING

On the map, Mexico resembles a great funnel, or rather, a cornucopia, with its widest part towards the north and its smallest end twisting to the south and east, meeting there the sudden expansion of the Maya area. There are few regions in the world with such a diverse geography as we find within this area – Mexico is not one, but many countries. All of the climatic extremes of our globe are found, from arctic cold near the summits of the highest volcanoes to the Turkish-bath atmosphere of the coastal jungles. Merely to pass from one valley to another is to enter a markedly different ecological zone.

This variation would be of interest only to the tourist agencies if one neglected to consider the effect of these contrasts upon man's occupation of Mexico. A topsy-turvy landscape of this sort means a similar diversity of the natural and cultivated products from region to region – above all, different crops with different harvest times. It means that no one region is now, or was in the past, truly self-sufficient. From the most remote antiquity, there has been an organic interdependence of one zone on the others, of one people or nation on all the rest. Thus, no matter how heterogeneous their languages or civilisations, the people of Mexico through exchange of products were bound up with each other into a single line of development; for this reason, great new advances were registered throughout the land within quite brief intervals of time.

Most of this funnel-shaped country lies above 3,000 feet, with really very little flat land. The Mexican highlands, our major concern in this book, are shaped by the mountain chains that swing down from the north, by the uplands between them, and by numerous volcanoes which have raised their peaks in fairly recent geological times. The western chain, the Sierra Madre Occidental, is the loftiest and broadest of these, being an extension of the Rocky Mountains; it and the Sierra Madre Oriental to the east enclose between their pine-clad ranges an immense inland plateau which is covered by mesquite-studded grasslands and occasionally even approaches true desert. Effectively outside the limits of Mesoamerican farming, the Mexican plateau was the homeland of barbarian hunters and collectors. As we move south, the two Sierras gradually approach each other until the interior wastelands terminate some 300 miles north of the Valley of Mexico.

Plate 1

The Valley of Mexico, the centre of the Aztec empire, is one of a number of natural basins in the midst of the Volcanic Cordillera, an extensive region of intense volcanism and frequent earthquakes. A mile and a half high with an area of 3,000 square miles, much of the Valley was once covered by a shallow lake of roughly figure-eight shape, now largely disappeared through ill-advised drainage and general desiccation of central Mexico in post-Conquest times. Since the Valley of Mexico has no outlet, changing rainfall patterns have produced severe fluctuations in the extent of the lake. As will be seen in Chapter VIII, the Aztec table was amply supplied by foods raised on its swampy margins in the misnamed 'floating gardens', or *chinampas*. Surrounded with hills on all sides, the Valley is dominated on the south-east by the snowy summits of the volcanoes Popocatépetl ('Smoking Mountain') and Iztaccíhuatl ('The White Lady').

Plate 2

Other important sections of the highlands are the Sierra Madre del Sur, its steep escarpment fronting the Pacific shoreline in southern Mexico, and the mountainous uplands of Oaxaca; both of these fuse to form a highland mass heavily dissected into countless valleys and ranges. Separated from this difficult country by the Isthmus of Tehuantepec,

international boundaries
limits of Mesoamerica
approximate western
limit of Maya Culture

Gulf of

Mexico

N

ulf of
mpeche

Yucatan
Peninsula

ain
sthmus
of
antepec

Rio Usumacinta

Rio Grijalva

BRITISH
HONDURAS

GUATEMALA

HONDURAS

EL
SALVADOR

Fig. 1   Map of major topographical features of Mexico

17

the south-eastern highlands form a continuous series of ranges from Chiapas down through Maya territory into lower Central America.

Although snow falls in some places at infrequent intervals, the Mexican highlands are temperate; before denudation by man, they were clothed in pines and cedars, with true boreal forests in the higher ranges. As elsewhere in Mexico, there are two strongly marked seasons – a winter dry period when rain seldom if ever falls, and a summer wet spell. The total rainfall is less than half that of the lowlands, so that occasionally conditions are arid and somewhat precarious for the farmer, in spite of the general richness of the soil. This is especially true of the boundary zone between the agricultural lands and the northern deserts.

The lowlands are confined to relatively narrow strips along the coasts, of which the most important is the plain fronting the Gulf of Mexico. Of alluvial origin, this band of flat land extends unbroken from Louisiana and Texas down through the Mexican states of Tamaulipas, Veracruz, and Tabasco to the Yucatan Peninsula, and played a critical role in the origins of settled life and the growth of civilisation in Mexico.

A bridge between the Gulf Coast Plain and the narrower and less humid Pacific Coast Plain is provided by the Isthmus of Tehuantepec, a constriction in the waist of Mesoamerica, with a gentle topography of low hills and sluggish rivers.

Lowland temperatures are thoroughly torrid throughout the year. So heavy is the summer precipitation that soils are generally red in colour and poor in mineral content as a result of drastic leaching. In most places, none the less, the dry season is well marked, so that many of the tropical trees lose their leaves in the winter. But where there is an unusually great amount of rain, one encounters the evergreen canopies and lush growth of the fully developed rain forest. Dotting the lowlands are patches of savannah grassland, sometimes quite extensive, and of no use to the ploughless Mexican farmer.

In response to the opportunities presented by these surroundings, contrasting modes of land cultivation have been developed over the millennia. Highland farmers are quite efficient about their land, since only a moderate period of fallowing is necessary for the fields, occasionally supplemented by manuring and a simple kind of irrigation. On the other hand, lowland cultivators, faced with immense forests, the low potential of the soil, and winter desiccation, have evolved a shifting form of horticulture which they share with other peoples throughout the tropics of the world. This system entails the cutting and burning of the forest from the plot to be sown; a very extensive territory is required for the support of each family since exhausted fields have to be left fallow for as much as ten years. Such a mode of food-getting could never have supported a large population, and we have every evidence to suggest a light occupation of the lowland zone throughout its history.

Tragically reduced in today's Mexico, game abounded in ancient times. The most important food animals are the white-tailed deer and the collared peccary, found everywhere. Confined to the lowlands are the tapir, the howler monkey, and the spider monkey, all of which are still eaten with relish by the native inhabitants. The lowlands also harbour the jaguar, the largest of the spotted cats and the source of much desired skins for the nobles of civilised Mexico; it must have been an object of primitive terror to the early dwellers of the coastal plains. Waterfowl, especially ducks, teem on the lakes and marshes of the uplands, and wild turkeys in the more isolated reaches of the country. Feathers from tropical birds such as the cotinga, the roseate spoonbill, the hummingbird, and above all, the quetzal, with iridescent blue-green plumage, provided rainbow-like splendour for head-dresses and other details of the costume.

There were no wild species in the New World suitable for domestication as draught animals. The native American horse was exterminated in the Ice Age by man; the South American llama is amenable only as a pack animal; and modern efforts to tame the North American bison have shown that beast to be completely intractable. As a consequence, none of the American Indians prior to their discovery had wheeled vehicles. Ancient Mexico did without any form of overland transportation other than the backs of men, although the principle of the wheel was known and applied to toys and idols of clay. The only warm-blooded animals kept in domestication were the dog and the turkey, the former as well as the latter valuable for its meat. Hives of tiny, stingless bees were exploited for honey by tropical lowlanders.

CLIMATE AND MAN IN MEXICO

High on the flanks of the hills fringing the Valley of Mexico are clearly visible the remains of beaches left by the great lake – from these alone it would be obvious that conditions in past times were very different from what they are today. A close study of pollen from weather-sensitive plants recovered from deep cores made in the Valley and elsewhere has revealed a long-term fluctuation in rainfall that may well have been a decisive factor in cultural changes on a broad scale.

To understand these fluctuations, we must go back in time more than two million years. Then, for reasons yet unknown, the generally warm and humid climate of the world suffered a profound change, and the Pleistocene, or Ice Age was initiated. Temperatures dropped and vast quantities of snow were deposited on the ever-rising mountain masses of far northern latitudes, to turn into massive ice sheets which ground their way south over much of northern Eurasia and North America. There were five or more of these glacial advances in the Pleistocene, separated by long interglacial periods during which more moderate conditions prevailed. In more southerly regions, such as Mexico, which actually lies within the Tropics, such advances of the northern ice are believed to have been reflected by pluvials, that is, by rainy, cool periods interspersed with dry intervals.

Fig. 2

Although geologists do not believe that we have ever really left the Pleistocene, an intense change took place at about 7000 BC, with the final retreat of the ice to the higher latitudes and the beginning of a long interval called the Hypsithermal in which world-wide temperatures were even higher than those of today. The Hypsithermal was broken by only one minor regrowth of the ice sheet in the northern reaches of Canada, the Cochrane Advance of about 5000 BC. From the second millennium before Christ until the present, the world has been in a 'Little Ice Age', with considerable glaciation in far northern climes and a fluctuating but generally greater rainfall than in the Hypsithermal.

These changes must have provided the parameters, the absolute limits, within which each way of life, each type of economy, must have had to operate in ancient Mexico. The period of the Early Hunters was a development of the late Pleistocene, when lush grasslands supported the large grazing animals which they killed and ate. With the switch to the relatively hot and dry climate of the Hypsithermal, the great herbivores had disappeared, and men had to adapt themselves to a new way of life, the Archaic, under semi-desert conditions in which every sort of plant

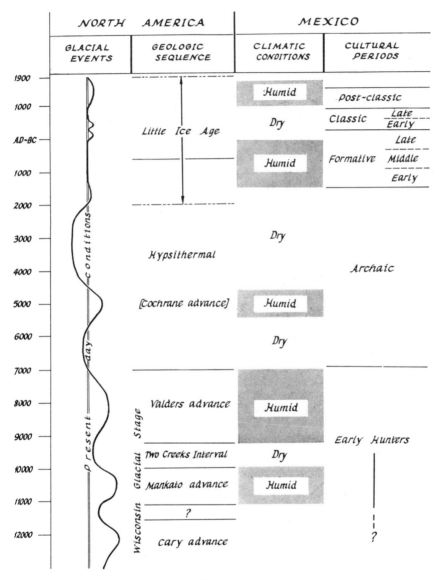

Fig. 2. Chart of cultural periods and changes of climate in Mexico

and animal food was systematically exploited. Men were forced to develop cunning and resourcefulness in the face of starvation. The sudden onset of wetter conditions about 1500 BC, with the prior domestication of food plants, set the stage for the established farming life of the Formative period. Although the height of Mexican civilisation was achieved during the Classic period (AD 300–900), the pollen profiles tell us that central Mexico, at least, became increasingly rainless, and it is more than a possibility that the premature Classic downfall there was due to successive droughts and crop failure. By the later part of the Post-Classic period, marked throughout its course by stepped-up military activities and the growth of conquest states, we have evidence of higher precipitation once more, when the great lake of the Valley of Mexico rose to an almost unprecedented level. The triumphant expansion of the Aztecs, ruling Mexico from their island capital near the western shore of the lake, may in part reflect such favourable conditions.

Full exploration of these suggestions will be left to the chapters which follow.

LANGUAGES AND PEOPLES

An amazing number of languages were spoken in native Mexico, a country of modest size. The situation would be even more confusing if it had not been for the efforts on the part of linguists to group them into families, of which some fourteen have been defined within the borders of our area.

Fig. 3

Of these, the largest and most important to the history of Mexico is Uto-Aztecan, comprising dozens of languages distributed from the north-western United States as far south as Panama. Since the greatest diversity within this family is found in far western Mexico, this wild region has been suggested as the probable heartland of the Uto-Aztecan peoples. By all odds the major language group within Uto-Aztecan is Nahua, the most significant dialect of which is Náhuatl, the language of the Aztecs and the *lingua franca* of their empire, still spoken by hundreds of thousands of farmers in the central Mexican highlands.

Other language families include Tarascan, the tongue of a large kingdom centred on Lake Pátzcuaro in the western part of the Volcanic Cordillera; Otomí-Pame, spoken by peoples who followed a semi-

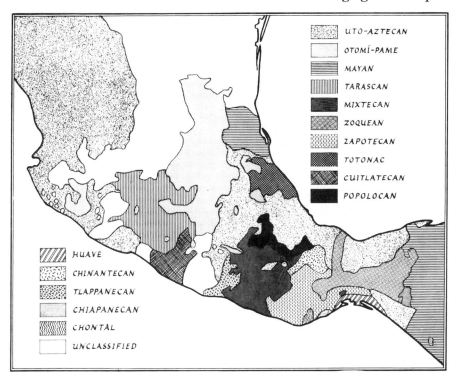

Legend:
- UTO-AZTECAN
- OTOMÍ-PAME
- MAYAN
- TARASCAN
- MIXTECAN
- ZOQUEAN
- ZAPOTECAN
- TOTONAC
- CUITLATECAN
- POPOLOCAN
- HUAVE
- CHINANTECAN
- TLAPPANECAN
- CHIAPANECAN
- CHONTAL
- UNCLASSIFIED

Fig. 3. Aboriginal language groups of Mexico at the time of the Spanish Conquest. Based on Mendizábal and Jiménez Moreno

barbarian way of life to the north of the Valley of Mexico, on the fringe of Mesoamerica; Totonac, spoken on the Gulf Coast, significantly in the region of the old Tajín civilisation; Mixtec and Zapotec, the dominant languages of the state of Oaxaca in southern Mexico; Zoquean, distributed from the Isthmus of Tehuantepec to the Grijalva Depression; and Huave, the language of primitive fishermen on the Pacific coast of the Isthmus. To the east is the large group of Mayan languages; this family has an enigmatic outlier, Huastec, in the area of the Gulf Coast north of the Totonac that is called, naturally enough, the Huasteca.

23

It would be a fruitless task to try to reconstruct Mexican history merely on the basis of these distributions. Nevertheless, it is evident that the expansion of Uto-Aztecan through much of Mexico must have been drastic; the isolated islands of Nahua speech as far south as lower Central America, Nahua place names, and the presence of Nahua words in many other languages testify to large-scale movements of peoples. We know in this case of Nahua conquests and migrations having taken place long before the imperialism of the Náhuatl-speaking Aztecs, events recorded in the traditional histories of these peoples. The role that they have played on the stage of New World history has certainly been in the grand style.

Other peoples have probably been more sedentary. But, contradictory as it may seem, while there is fairly good knowledge of the geographic position of most language groups in Mexico at the time of the Conquest, archaeologists are often loth to apply linguistic names to past civilisations unless they are sure beyond any doubt of the identification, as in the case of the Maya, whose writings we have, or the Aztecs. Stones and pottery fragments do not tell us who made them, so that we must be content with the non-committal names which archaeologists have given us for past peoples.

CHAPTER II

Early Hunters

While the broad outline of what happened during the late Pleistocene in the New World is becoming clearer with every new discovery of very early artifacts and sites, it is still not established exactly when man first entered this hemisphere. The *how* is almost indisputable. The last major stage of the Pleistocene, the Wisconsin in North America, began around 50,000 years ago and continued, with many fluctuations, until 9,000 years ago. Because their water was taken up into ice, the oceans of the world during the advances of the late Wisconsin were 200 feet lower than they stand at present, sufficiently exposing a platform to form a land bridge at least 1,000 miles wide between Siberia and the western coast of Alaska. Although an enormous sheet of ice then covered much of North America as far south as the Great Lakes of today, the land bridge was ice-free, as was western Alaska and the Yukon valley. The earliest migrant hunters into America would then have crossed from Asia through a tundra-covered, treeless, cold region, covered with thin and patchy snows in winter.

Fig. 2

All of the early skeletons which we have from the Early Hunters stage indicate that these peoples were ancestral American Indians belonging to the great Mongoloid branch of mankind; no remains of Peking Man, Neanderthal, or any other archaic form of our genus have ever been discovered in this hemisphere. Since *Homo sapiens* arose in the Old World no earlier than the final glacial stage, and because no indisputably Last Interglacial artifacts have come to light in North or South America, we may safely assume that man must have entered Alaska during the Wisconsin. Rising sea levels beginning at about 8000 BC would have drowned the most feasible entry route, so that migrations must have predated this. Most archaeologists would lean to an *early* Wisconsin date for the most ancient migrations, which probably continued for a considerable period of time.

Some recent finds tend to back up this 'long chronology' for man's entry into the hemisphere. At Valsequillo, near Puebla in southern

Fig. 4

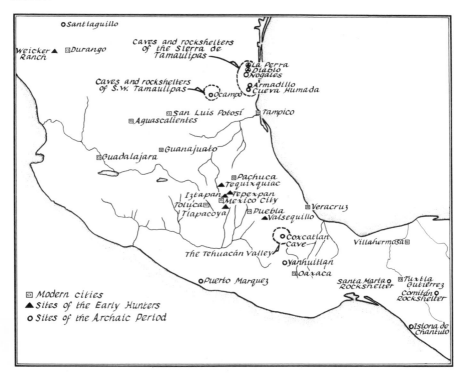

Fig. 4. Sites of the Early Hunters and the Archaic Periods

Mexico, Cynthia Irwin-Williams has found cultural remains associated with an extinct fauna which included mammoth, mastodon, horse, antelope, dire wolf, and smaller mammals; the lack of bifacially worked projectile points suggests a very early date, confirmed by a radiocarbon determination of about 21,000 years ago. In the Valley of Mexico itself, dates ranging from 21,000 to 24,000 years ago have been established at the island site of Tlapacoya for a crude industry of choppers, scrapers, flakes, and a blade and burin. Ranging into the earliest known occupation of South America, Dr Richard MacNeish has found in a highland Peruvian cave near Ayacucho an equally crude and very similar industry dated between 16,000 and 21,000 years before the present. The time perspective might be pushed back even further by William Irving's find on the Yukon of fossil bone tools with dates ranging from 26,000 to 29,000 years ago; and most recently, by three human skeletons from southern California which have been placed by the new but still controversial amino-acid racemisation technique at 48,000 years ago!

The New World must have been an untouched paradise for the first hunting people. Extensive herds of large grazing animals such as mammoths, mastodons, camels, horses, and giant bison roamed through both subcontinents. With ideal conditions such as these, population expansion and spread were probably fairly rapid. Radiocarbon dating has demonstrated that men were hunting sloth, horse, and guanaco at the Straits of Magellan by at least 9000 B C, and there is a reasonable possibility that most of South America was populated long before this.

To understand the significance of finds of late Pleistocene date that have been made in Mexico, it is necessary to consider them in the light of the Early Hunters stage as we now know it for North America as a whole, especially for the United States, where research on this problem has been most intensive. The consensus of opinion of New World archaeologists is that the earliest known remains are those of a very simple culture of hunters and gatherers in which the majority of tools were inconceivably crude, percussion chipped, pebble artifacts. Coarse choppers, chopping tools, scrapers, and knives are found at a number of campsites and open stations in the western United States under conditions of great antiquity; since this rudimentary inventory is exactly that of the late Pleistocene population of east Asia, it is believed to represent the non-perishable part of the tool-kit of the first immigrants.

By approximately 10,000 B C an immense technological change had taken place, with the introduction or invention of fine percussion- and pressure-flaked stone points of the type known as Clovis. These have, extending up from the base on one or both sides, a broad channel or flute formed by the removal of long, narrow flakes by a technique that is not yet well understood. Clovis points are found over much of North America, from Alaska down to Panama; some magnificent specimens come from mammoth 'kill' sites in Arizona near the Mexican border. In the American South-west, at about 8000 B C, a refinement in fluting produced the well-known Folsom point; specimens of this type

cf. Fig. 5

cf. Fig. 6

supersede Clovis, and are often associated with bison 'kills'. All of these points, because of their size and weight, are considered to be the 'business end' of darts which were hurled with the aid of a spearthrower (or *atlatl*, to use the Náhuatl term). The bow and arrow was a late arrival in Mexico and was not adopted at all in many areas.

Concurrently with Folsom, which has a somewhat restricted distribution, in the Great Plains as far south as Texas appeared a number of related industries all characterised by bifacially chipped, lanceolate points (Angostura, Scottsbluff, etc.); in actuality, this lanceolate point 'horizon' covers much of Latin America as well. The origin of the techniques and concepts involved in the production of bifacially chipped dart and lance points in this hemisphere is not known, although some have looked to the Old World where very similar industries have existed from a much earlier time level.

Of course, all of the above-mentioned tool inventories were the equipment of peoples who were without agriculture and who lived mainly by the chase and the gathering of wild plant foods. From what we know about still extant societies with a similar way of life, such as the Australian aborigines, concentrations of population larger than the small band were quite impossible. Edward Deevey has estimated that on this level of development, corresponding roughly to the Upper Palaeolithic of Europe, 25 square miles of territory are required for the support of one person. In all the New World prior to 7000 B C there may never have been at any one moment in time more than half a million persons, with about 30,000 of these in Mexico – a crude guess, to be sure, but not unreasonable.

Late Pleistocene Mexico presented a landscape considerably different from that which we see at the present. Rain poured then on places where it hardly touches today, and many semi-deserts must have been in those remote times a sea of grass. The great lake in the Valley of Mexico, where the most significant finds of the Early Hunters stage have been found, was a great deal broader and deeper, as testified by old strand lines on the surrounding hills.

Fig. 5

A single dart point of the Clovis type of quartzite, about two inches long, was found on the surface of the Weicker Ranch, some 30 miles west of the city of Durango in north-western Mexico. Like all Clovis specimens, this is a fluted point fashioned by a combination of

*Fig. 5. Clovis point from the
Weicker ranch, Durango. 1/4*

percussion- and pressure-flaking and shows the characteristic dulling of
the edges at the sides and base (presumably to prevent abrasion of the
lashing by which it was bound to the shaft). By analogy with radiocarbon-dated Clovis sites in the United States, this artifact represents an
occupation of Mexico as early as the tenth millennium B C.

Fresh-water sediments over 250 feet thick underlie Mexico City and
all areas of the now dry beds of the great lake in the Valley of Mexico.
Geological work has established a stratigraphy for the upper part of these
deposits that corresponds to the later part of the Pleistocene and all of the
post-Pleistocene climatic sequence. Crucial to the problem of the ancient
occupation in the Valley is the Becerra Formation, divided into an
Upper and a Lower. The latter probably pertains to the early or middle
Wisconsin Stage, while the Upper Becerra Formation can be assigned
with some confidence to the Valders Advance (9000–7000 B C), on the
basis of a single radiocarbon date and the kind of artifacts associated with
this stratum.

The Upper Becerra is a fine, green muck, and has lenses of ash
deposited by the volcanoes that were then in frequent eruption. Over this
is a layer of brown, sandy sediments that were deposited at a time when
the great lake was shrinking. Presumably this layer represents the first
part of the Hypsithermal Interval, broken by the sudden readvance of the
Cochrane ice in Canada. A turn to really dry conditions and
desiccation of the lake bed is indicated by a layer of *caliche*, or calcium
carbonate, marking the climax of the Hypsithermal. From the *caliche*
layer to the surface are several layers which probably date from the late
Hypsithermal to modern times and which contain abundant potsherds.

As long ago as 1870 the Mexican naturalist Barcena discovered the
sacrum of an extinct llama which had been carved to represent the head
of an animal, apparently a large member of the dog family, at the locality

Plate 3

of Tequixquiac, 42 miles north of Mexico City. This specimen lay at a depth of 40 feet below the surface, in deposits of unknown age. One can only indulge in guesswork, but several other lesser finds at Tequixquiac in recent years have been ascribed to the base of the Upper Becerra Formation, and the carved sacrum may well have been found in this layer.

Few finds in recent years in Mexico have aroused such general interest as the famous 'Tepexpan Man'. In 1949 the geologist Helmut de Terra was engaged in a search for mammoth skeletons in the vicinity of Tepexpan, on the north-eastern edge of the old beds of Lake Texcoco, a locality known to be rich in Pleistocene fossils. Almost as an accidental by-product of his survey, a human skeleton was exposed in one trench. 'Tepexpan Man' appears to have been deliberately buried by his fellows, face down and with the legs drawn up under the body, unaccompanied by any offerings. According to a recent study by Dr Santiago Genovés, the dead person was a woman of no more than 30 years of age, about 160 cms. (5 ft. 2 in.) tall, and not particularly different from Mexican Indians in general. The major problem about 'Tepexpan Man', it should be unequivocally stressed, is the actual stratigraphic position of the skeleton when discovered. According to De Terra, it was found in the Upper Becerra formation, a stratum known to have fossil elephant remains as well, and underlying the *caliche*. Unfortunately, the inept handling of the excavation makes it unlikely that we shall ever know whether this was so or not. As Marie Wormington has pointed out, the type of burial represented by 'Tepexpan Man' suggests the subsequent Archaic Period, when flexed, unaccompanied interments are common, at least in the United States. However, fluorine tests recently carried out have pretty well demonstrated the contemporaneity of the skeleton with mammalian fossils known to be of Upper Becerra age. 'Tepexpan Man' may be our First Mexican, after all.

Far more satisfactory and less enigmatic results have been obtained on the old lake flats near Santa Isabel Iztápan, only a few kilometres south of Tepexpan. In 1952, Mexican prehistorians, following up a chance find by workers opening a drainage ditch, excavated the skeleton of an imperial mammoth (*Mammuthus imperator*) which lay entirely within the green muck of the Upper Becerra Formation, and which was therefore Valders in age. The animal had been butchered *in situ*, a fact which

Plate 4

could be deduced from the disarticulated position of the bones alone. Most importantly, six human artifacts were indisputably associated with the skeleton. These included a flint projectile point of the type known as Scottsbluff, one of the most widely distributed artifacts of the lanceolate point horizon on the Great Plains of the United States. The other artifacts were utilised in cutting up the mammoth, and comprised a scraper, knife, and fine prismatic blade, all of obsidian, and an end scraper and retouched blade of flint.

Fig. 6

In 1954, the construction of another ditch by the Santa Isabel Iztápan villagers resulted in the lucky find of a second mammoth 'kill', again with artifacts which had been lost during the butchering process. Here a hind leg of the animal had been caught in the Upper Becerra muck, probably as it was fleeing its human pursuers. During the butchering process, the head and tusks had been dragged back across the body, and some bones showed deep cuts made by stone knives while the meat was being hacked off. Three chipped stone artifacts found among the bones comprise an Angostura point of a dark igneous material, a Lerma point of flint, and a chert, bifacially worked knife. The first two named are of some interest. Angostura points also can be ascribed to the lanceolate point horizon on the Great Plains, known to be later than the Clovis horizon. Lerma points have an even wider spread in the late Wisconsin Glacial, being found in Texas and north-eastern Mexico (where they appear as early as 8000 B C), and are one of the most common types of point ascribed to the Early Hunters stage in South America as far south as Argentina. We have no radiocarbon dates on the Santa Isabel Iztápan finds, but charcoal from a hearth next to a skeleton of still another slaughtered mammoth in the same formation has been dated to 7710 B C ± 400 by this process.

Plate 5

Fig. 6

We can reconstruct something of the life and environment of these lacustrine hunters of the Valley of Mexico some 10,000 years ago, although it must be remembered that we lack all knowledge of their campsites and have the chance evidence only of their hunting prowess. The climate was more humid and cooler than that of today; in fact, the now barren outskirts of the Valley were covered with pine forests. In the distance, the young cones of the active volcanoes poured out smoke, ash, and lava, perhaps disturbing the tempo of life in the Valley from time to time, but not seriously disrupting it. The imperial mammoth seems to

cf. Fig. 2

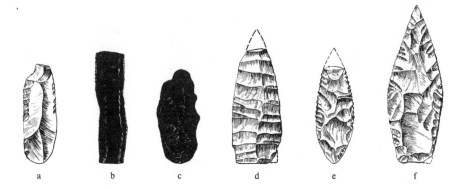

Fig. 6. Chipped stone tools found in association with mammoths at Santa Isabel Iztápan. a, flint retouched blade; b, obisidian prismatic blade; c, obsidian knife; d, flint Scottsbluff point; e, flint Lerma point; f, Angostura point. 1/2

have favoured the swampy margins of the wide, shallow lake. These beasts must have been relatively easy game to organized groups of hunters, who, armed with darts hurled from atlatls and equipped with stone knives and other butchering tools, drove the heavy beasts into shallower water where they became hopelessly mired in the treacherous lake bottom. There each mammoth was isolated and dispatched, although probably not without danger as the risk of impalement by the formidable tusks of the surrounded animal must have been considerable – to kill any elephant with spears would require pluck.

On the north-eastern frontier of Mexico, in the state of Tamaulipas, Richard S. MacNeish has revealed in his excavations a long cultural sequence that begins with our primitive Hunters and Gatherers. The earliest of these phases, the Diablo Complex, is of some simplicity, comprising only crude, bifacially flaked and uniface tools made from flints or pebbles; choppers, ovoid blades, pebble end-scrapers, and crude flake side-scrapers suggest an unspecialised hunting and gathering way of life on the most rudimentary level. Since these artifacts are found in a high terrace of the Canyon Diablo, formed when the river was running very much higher and the climate was obviously much wetter than today, MacNeish has suggested that the Diablo Complex be contemporaneous with the Mankato Advance, 11–10,000 B C.

Plate 6

A far better picture of Ice Age life in Mexico comes from the Tehuacán Valley in Puebla, where a large-scale project directed by MacNeish has disclosed a late Pleistocene occupation called the Ajuereado phase. Radiocarbon dates suggest that it ended about 6500 B C, but it must have been in part coeval with the Tepexpan kills. The evidence shows that the climate was cooler and drier than that now prevailing, with open steppe covering the valley floor. In this setting grazed subsequently extinct horse and pronghorn antelope, which were hunted with spears fitted with Lerma points. The inhabitants also sought smaller game, such as jack rabbits, gophers, and rats. The tool technology was totally based upon chipped stone; in addition to projectile points, there were knives, choppers, side-scrapers (for dressing hides), and crude blades. Ground stone tools, which could have been used to prepare vegetable foods, are absent, although some wild plants such as prickly pear cactus and *Setaria* grass were surely harvested by crude means.

The inhabitants of Tehuacán during Ajuereado times were probably grouped into about three nomadic families or microbands of four to eight people each, and the evidence of cave floor occupations shows that camps were changed three or four times a season, since there never was enough food in any one ecological niche to support settled life, a state of affairs which also prevailed throughout the succeeding Archaic stage.

Fig. 7

Fig. 7. Probable community patterns, Ajuereado phase in the Tehuacán Valley. Groups moved from wet-season camps (circles), to fall camps (squares), to dry-season camps (triangles).

33

It would be a dangerous misconception to consider this period, viewed as a whole, as merely the time when men hunted huge Pleistocene animals such as mammoth, horse, and so forth. As a matter of fact, in actual habitation sites of this date in Texas and elsewhere in the United States, the vast majority of animal bones come from relatively small animals, as humble as rodents, snakes, snails, and mussels. These people gathered and ate everything that was edible, and probably had to survive some very lean seasons. Since most of the sites which we have are large and conspicuous 'kills', we have been deluded into thinking that we are dealing with some sort of ancient 'big game hunters' who disdained smaller animals or plant foods. True, large herbivores were slaughtered, but from this we must not assume that the late Pleistocene was a time of plenty. Like the modern Pygmies of the African rain forest, who also hunt elephants, success in the chase probably meant a short feast marked by voracious gluttony, with long intervals of eating whatever they could lay their hands on.

CHAPTER III

The Archaic Period

Six thousand years of almost uninterruptedly high temperatures, as much as 2° C (3·6° F) above present averages in some places, set in on the heels of the Valders ice advance, around 7000 B C. Of course, within this span there were minor fluctuations such as the Cochrane Advance in North America at about 5000 B C, and near 2000 B C the first sporadic indications of a 'Little Ice Age'. The pleasant term 'Climatic Optimum' has been invented for this Hypsithermal period in western Europe, for there the inhabitants of the lands facing on the Atlantic enjoyed significantly wetter as well as warmer weather, perhaps the most balmy ever seen in those regions. Such favourable conditions hardly obtained elsewhere in the world, and in North America this long interval was largely one of desiccation. In contrast to the oak forests of humid Europe, vast areas of the New World were transformed into desert wastes.

Fig. 2

Odd though it may seem, during the Hypsithermal, men continued to live throughout even the most desiccated zones of North America. Species after species of large game animal perished not long after its onset – mastodon, mammoth, horse, camel, giant bison, ground sloth, dire wolf, etc. – but the Indian survived. New tools, new hunting methods, other sources of food, perhaps different forms of shelter, all these enabled men to adapt to radically altered conditions of life, whereas other species were trapped by the extreme slowness of the rate of biological, as opposed to cultural, evolution.

The new stage of cultural adaptation attained by man in the New World is called the Archaic, and it is the full equivalent of the Mesolithic stage in the western part of the Old World. Denied the rich hunting economy of their late Pleistocene predecessors, small bands of Indians concentrated on more efficient methods of killing smaller game, on fishing and gathering of molluscs, and to an ever-increasing extent on the collection of specific plant foods.

Fig. 4

Mexico

THE DESERT CULTURE IN NORTH AMERICA

In the dry semi-deserts of the Great Basin and south-western United States, these Archaic hunters and collectors inhabited caves and open sites near the ever-dwindling lakes or by seepages of water. The pattern which enabled men to eke out a livelihood in this inhospitable environment has been named the Desert Culture, which persisted into the nineteenth century among the nomadic Indians of the Great Basin. Its salient features include a sparse population with no groups larger than the band; caves and rock shelters favoured for settlements; a subsistence pattern based on the seasonal exploitation of humble food resources such as rabbits, wild plant seeds, and even insects; preparation of plant foods by grinding them on a flat milling stone with a cobble *mano*; abundant basketry, matting, and sandals (known as early as 7000 B C in caves in Oregon); darts tipped with relatively small, percussion-chipped points and hurled by means of the atlatl; a wide variety of scrapers, choppers, scraper planes, and so forth, of remarkably crude manufacture; and the dog, present for the first time in North America early in this development.

cf. Fig. 8

It now appears that the Desert Culture pattern is far more widespread in North America than was once thought. Similar Archaic remains are known all the way from Oregon, through the Great Basin and South-west, including Texas, and now as far south in Mexico as the Guatemalan border. The region that concerns us here, Mexico, must have been extraordinarily hot and dry, as shown by known shrinking of the great lake of the Valley of Mexico and by the overwhelming appearance of dry pollen indicators in the cores at this time.

The discovery in recent years of an Archaic period of Desert Culture type in Mexico has unexpectedly thrown light on one of the great problems in New World archaeology: where, when, and how were the major food plants domesticated by the American Indian? For it was the cultivation of maize, beans, and squash that made possible all of the higher cultures of Mexico, and, to a certain degree, those of Peru as well. In the effort to bridge the gap between the ancient hunting peoples and the first indications of full-blown village life, the researches of Richard S. MacNeish have produced particularly important results, described in this chapter.

There is no simple definition of the term *domestication*. Quite obviously, there is a difference between the domestication of an animal like the dog or pig, which can and often do revert to the 'wild' state, and a creature, the reproduction of which entirely depends upon the presence of man, such as the dromedary camel. We are clearly dealing here with a broad spectrum, in which the *degree* of domestication may vary widely; one might thus adopt the definition proposed many years ago by the Russian geneticist Vavilov, and say that it is evolution directed by the interference of man. Basically, this implies that man has in some systematic way tampered with the reproduction of a certain species, a process which may be totally unwitting.

As in animals, in its most extreme form plant domestication ends up with species which cannot reproduce by themselves and which are therefore without wild populations. In the case of cereals and other plants which reproduce by means of seeds, this implies that artificial selection by man has resulted in species which lack the ability to disperse their seeds. Not until that state has been reached can botanists be sure of the presence of domestication in ancient plant remains. It is no accident that all of the important food plants of the world belong in this category of totally captive populations, since the reduction of the ability to self-reproduce has resulted in greatly increased food values in the plants concerned.

THE IMPORTANCE OF MAIZE

The Aztecs believed that their hero-god Quetzalcóatl, who created mankind with his own blood, turned himself into an ant so as to be able to steal a single grain of maize which the ants had hidden inside a mountain; this he gave to men so that they might be nourished. Maize was and is the very basis of settled life in Mexico and, in fact, throughout the regions of the New World civilised in Pre-Columbian times. Speculation as to the origin of this staple has therefore been freely indulged in, with many theories proposed which are no more firmly grounded than the Aztec myth recorded above.

An older generation of archaeologists was raised in the belief that the story of the domestication of maize was completely known. Since maize (*Zea mays*) is a grass with no known wild forms, the search was early started for a closely related species in the wild state. In the highlands of Chiapas and Guatemala, very near the heart of the so-called 'Old Empire' of the Maya, a grass called *teosinte* grows in and near Indian cornfields as an unwanted weed; this species is clearly affiliated in some way with maize, most botanists placing it within the same genus. It was very early claimed that this was the wild ancestor of maize, and that the process of taming it to meet man's needs was the achievement of the notably advanced Maya. From these people maize was supposed to have spread, along with the arts of civilisation, far and wide throughout the New World. This story is very neat, but it unfortunately has not met the test of modern plant genetics and experimental breeding. The researches of Paul C. Mangelsdorf and his colleagues later suggested that *teosinte* is not the mother of maize, but its daughter, the result of a hybridisation between domesticated maize and a truly wild relative, tripsacum (*Zea tripsacum*), an event which must have taken place, if it took place at all, rather late in the history of maize.

The supposed exclusion of *teosinte* from the picture turned the attention of botanists elsewhere. These researches have settled on a strange variety of maize called pod corn, which turns up as a kind of weird sport in primitive cornfields in South America. The kernels of pod corn, unlike those of modern maize, are completely enclosed in glumes, or chaff; furthermore, the ripe ear is only partly covered by husks and therefore may disperse its seeds without the aid of man – a contrast to the 'captive' maize. It was felt that the ancestor of maize must have had many of the characteristics of pod corn, as well as some of the features of pop corn which is primitive in having small, hard seeds (this is the reason why it has to be popped). Experiments in crossing modern pod corn with pop corn revealed the true nature of the hereditary factors involved in the domestication of maize, as well as some of the more probable features which this hypothetical ancestor must have possessed. The wild progenitor was apparently a small plant with a single stalk and a single inflorescence at the top – that is, a female flower (ear) which bore the seeds after fertilisation, and a male flower (tassel) at the top. The plant would have been self-fertilising, of course, and like pod corns today had heavy chaff covering the kernels, but greatly reduced husks.

Apparently a single mutation was responsible for many changes in the plant, a genetic alteration which resulted in multiple effects. The primary change was a reduction in glumes or chaff, releasing energy for the production of a larger cob with more and larger kernels. This mutation also lowered the position of the inflorescences, or flowers, and it is known that the lower the ear, the stronger the stalk, with a greater capacity for producing larger ears; the more likely it is to develop only female flowers which produce kernels when pollinated (the male tassel remains at the top of the plant); and the longer the shanks attaching the ear to the stalk – shanks which give rise to more husks surrounding the ear. The end result of this mutation is a plant which is not adapted to wild conditions.

Here is where man must have stepped in. A group of primitive collectors of plant food might have favoured wild maize plants which exhibited the larger ears and brought the harvest back to their camps, some of the seeds eventually ending up in the messy refuse heaps which accompany this sort of life. Thus, the mutants would have been captured by man and artificially selected by him – a form of conscious and unconscious domestication together. Once these Indians learned that the plants would produce better if the plots were cleared of weeds, new avenues in the improvement of maize were opened. One might logically ask, but why did wild maize become extinct? Some botanists believe that domesticated maize backcrossed with wild populations so frequently in early history that the latter were eliminated by taking on the mutant gene resulting in non-dispersal of seeds. In like manner, continued back-crossing between *teosinte* and maize in modern Indian fields is bringing these two kinds of *Zea* so close to one another that many taxonomists now place them as members of the same species.

Where did these events take place? Botanists have fluctuated in their search from Mesoamerica to South America, and some have leaned to multiple points of origin in the New World. Preposterous claims of maize origins in Asia, Africa, or the Near East may be dismissed. Fossil evidence casting light on this problem comes from a core made in the Valley of Mexico. At a depth of 200 feet, in deposits which must be at least 80,000 years old and which therefore certainly predate man's presence there, were found pollen grains which demonstrate conclusively that wild maize was in Mexico by this date. To the north of Mesoamerica proper, in a rock-shelter called Bat Cave in south central New Mexico, charred cobs of an exceptionally primitive kind of maize have been found along with pre-pottery remains of Desert Culture aspect, all dating to about 2500 BC. The plant was apparently domesticated, but the cobs are no larger than a strawberry; it seems that these represent a very early stage in the domestication process. Thus, North rather than South America, and more specifically the region in and near Mexico, would seem to hold the answer which has been sought for so long. It is this likelihood which has made more recent work in Mexico so interesting.

OTHER CULTIGENS

While maize is at the centre of the Mesoamerican food complex, other vegetable foods always accompany it. Of these, beans are the most significant. The common bean (*Phaseolus vulgaris*), known in a great many varieties today, is the most popular in Mexican diets and presumably has been so since very early periods. On the basis of a distribution of wild forms, Vavilov suggested a primary domestication in Mexico or Guatemala. Of squashes, there are three major species in Mexico; *Cucurbita pepo* (pumpkin), *C. moschata* (warty or crookneck squash), and *C. mixta* (walnut squash), the forms of all of which are virtually legion, as any visitor to a Mexican food market can testify. The origins of all of these from wild ancestors or through hybridisation are very little understood, although the sequence of their appearance in Mexico is now established. The same might be said of chili peppers (*Capsicum* sp.), now the major ingredient in 'hot' foods the world over, but of Mexican and Peruvian origin; the major problem with this seasoning (also an important source of vitamins to Indian populations) is the difficulty of distinguishing between wild and domesticated seeds.

CAVES AND ROCK-SHELTERS OF NORTH-EASTERN MEXICO

Tamaulipas is the north-easternmost state of Mexico, and as such is on the very edge of Mesoamerica as we have defined it here. Because of the rainless, almost semi-desert environment, the tribes encountered by the Spaniards in this backward region were, with few exceptions, hunters and collectors without knowledge of cultivation. The aridity of Tamaulipas has meant ideal conditions of preservation in cave and rock-shelter sites, of which a good many have been discovered. MacNeish has concentrated his excavations in two zones, the Sierra de Tamaulipas, an isolated and highly dissected upland, and south-western Tamaulipas, on the very dry, eastern slope of the Sierra Madre Oriental. Of these two, the former was by far the most favourable for ancient settlement, and sites are accordingly more frequent there.

SIERRA DE TAMAULIPAS

Five stratified rock-shelters have been tested in the Sierra de Tamaulipas, of which the most rewarding were Diablo Canyon at the base of a 150-foot high cliff; La Perra Cave, in the same canyon but north of Diablo Cave; and Nogales Cave, perched in a cliff about five miles south of Diablo Cave. All of these rock-shelters are mere recesses far above the stream beds but connected to them by broad talus slopes. In the established sequence, the most ancient phases, Diablo and Lerma, belong to the Early Hunters period and have already been described.

Plate 6

The Archaic period opens here with the Nogales phase, estimated to last from 5000 to *c.* 3000 BC, and having developed during dry conditions much like those prevailing today. In the Nogales phase and throughout the Sierra de Tamaulipas Archaic, one finds crude tools for butchering, preparation of hides or woodworking: scrapers, choppers, ovoid blades, pebble hammerstones, disk scrapers, gouges, scraping planes, as well as certain atlatl dart points. The last-named comprise a number of types well known in arid North America, particularly in Texas; the Nogales types include some left over from the Early Hunters period, such as Lerma and Plainview points, along with purely Archaic points like the round-based Abasolo, and the more triangular Nogales and Tortugas types. Some of these show traces of resin with which their bases were fixed to dart shafts. Preservation is poor in Nogales occupation levels, but mortars, pestles, manos and crude querns indicate that collection and grinding of wild seeds may have been the major source of food. There was also extensive hunting, especially of deer, coatimundi and jaguar. Shell beads are the only indications of costume.

Fig. 10

Fig. 9

Fig. 8

La Perra deposits overlie those of Nogales, and here we are blessed with almost perfect preservation, in fact some might say too perfect as the inhabitants of these rock-shelters had only scanty notions of hygiene. A single radiocarbon date has enabled MacNeish to estimate its duration

Fig. 8. Characteristic ground stone tools of the Archaic in Tamaulipas. a, mortar; b, hand stone or mano; c, milling stone. 1/4

Fig. 11

from 3000 to about 2200 BC. The abundant stone tools carry on traditions already present in Nogales. From the La Perra dust MacNeish also extracted fragments of simple coiled nets, checker-twilled mats, stitch and wrap coiled baskets, dart shafts tipped with stone points (usually Tortugas) set in gum, and many kinds of knots tied in S-twisted string, all cordage being made from the fibres of wild plants like yucca and agave.

Fairly accurate estimates can be made of the importance of various food-getting activities in the subsistence of the La Perra people. Only 15 per cent of the food eaten came from the chase, principally deer, peccary, and jaguar. Somewhat surprisingly, as much as 76 per cent of the diet was of vegetable origin, including nuts, seeds, and cactus fruits; fibrous plants were chewed, thoroughly masticated quids appearing frequently in the refuse (a good Desert Culture trait). Even grasshoppers and other insects were collected and eaten raw, as testified by remains in faeces. Nine per cent of La Perra subsistence was the result of plant cultivation. La Perra maize was a tiny-eared pop corn with, as might be expected, many pod corn characteristics, and is slightly more domesticated than that of Bat Cave, which may predate it. An analysis of the cobs shows that it was eaten in several ways: (1) chewing soon after pollination, to suck out the sugar-rich juices; (2) as green corn roasted in the ear; (3) as pop corn; and (4) as a cooked dough or gruel prepared by grinding the ripe ear and kernels on a metate. Pumpkin (*Cucurbita pepo*) was also grown in La Perra gardens, both seeds and flesh being eaten raw.

The succeeding Almagre phase yielded little else but a series of stone artifacts, with the addition of some new projectile points which again are well known in the Archaic of Texas. The old mode of life must have continued, with ever-increasing reliance on cultivation, but preservation of plant remains is absent. An intensification of food production appears to have results in modest villages of wattle-and-daub houses, from the evidence of two sites of Almagre affiliation. By its close, estimated at 1500 BC, Mexico itself had already entered into a completely settled village life.

SOUTH-WESTERN TAMAULIPAS

The very first cultivated plants appear even earlier in South-western Tamaulipas, where a more severe desiccation of the zone has had the effect of providing a stratified sequence of beautifully preserved materials. In truth, the caves around Ocampo are a sort of Valley of the Kings on the lowest level of development. Furthermore, even more radiocarbon dates are available. The earliest phase, Infiernillo, with dates of 6544 BC and 6244 BC ± 450, and therefore just post-Valders in age, is typically Archaic, with many of the Desert Culture hallmarks already noted for this region, emphasising the same range of tool types and perishable artifacts (atlatl and dart fragments, nets, twined baskets, and mats).

To the astonishment of all, the plants present included the domesticated bottle gourd (*Lagenaria siceraria*), thus making it the most ancient cultigen of the New World. It turns up at a somewhat later date on the Peruvian coast. The history of the bottle gourd, usable only as a container since the meat is usually inedible, is puzzling. It is believed by botanists to be of Old World origin, probably with an initial centre of domestication in Africa. Tests have shown that the seeds are viable after the dried gourd has been immersed for several years in sea water. Accordingly, the likelihood is that the plant floated from Africa to the New World to land on some eastern shore. How, then, did the American Indian adopt it as his own? It is suggested as remotely possible that some beachcomber of a distant era came across a gourd by accident, carried it back to his camp and sowed the seeds. One needs hardly to stress that this reconstruction is pure fantasy, but we are hardly prepared to adopt the alternative explanation, namely that African voyagers carried the gourd with them on a sea trip to the west at this early date.

Other plants in the Infiernillo phase include pumpkin, some of the seeds of which appear to be definitely wild, runner beans (*Phaseolus coccineus*) and chili peppers. None of these can with confidence be stated

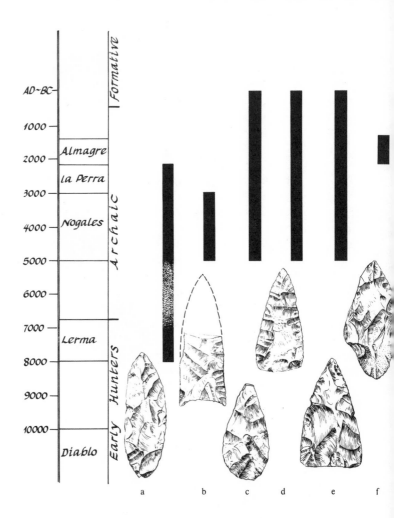

to be domesticated in Infiernillo, although the pumpkin may be just on the verge through systematic collection of certain mutants.

Radiocarbon dates on the succeeding Ocampo phase range from 3694 BC to 2624 BC ± 350, establishing it as contemporary with both Nogales and La Perra. Hunting had decreased in importance as food collection increased. More unequivocally domesticated plants are present, comprising bottle gourd, pumpkin, two varieties of common

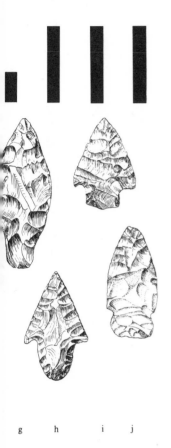

g   h   i   j

Fig. 9. Sequence of stone projectile points in Tamaulipas. The vertical bars indicate the extent in time of each. a, Lerma; b, Plainview; c, Abasolo; d, Nogales; e, Tortugas; f, Almagre; g, Kent; h, Gary; i, Palmillas; j, Ensor. 1/2

beans, and chili peppers. Undigested fragments of maize plants have been identified in faeces, but with this sort of data conclusions can hardly be drawn as to whether these plants were domesticated or not.

The Flacco phase follows Ocampo and develops directly from it; it is radiocarbon-dated to about 2000 BC, contemporary with Almagre. While semi-nomadic food-collecting was still the dominant mode of subsistence, hunting had dwindled to a point where it provided less food

45

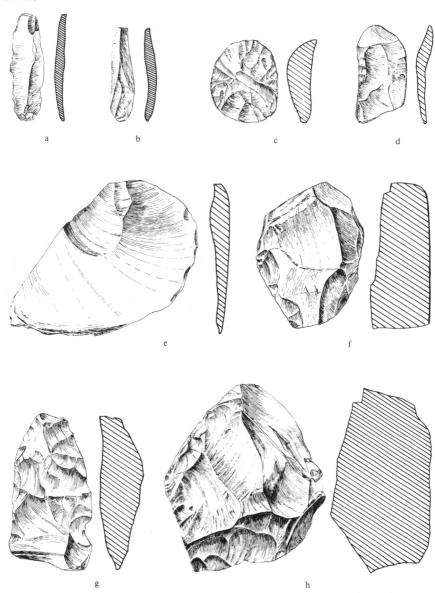

a

b

c

d

e

f

g

h

than the developing techniques of cultivation. Maize, squash, gourds, chili pepper, and common beans were grown, while wild millet (*Panicum* sp.), amaranths, and runner beans were perhaps collected but not sown.

Dating to the very threshold of the Formative period, the Guerra phase is already semi-sedentary. Now, cultivation overshadows all other modes of livelihood, and maize cobs are the most abundant plant-remains encountered. Along with all of the other cultigens already seen, cotton makes its appearance. It is likely that the Guerra people already occupied small villages, the first tentative approaches towards settled life in north-eastern Mexico.

The two regional sequences established here in Tamaulipas have bridged the gap of many millennia that separates the hunters of the Pleistocene and the very first pottery-using peasants of the Formative period. As a result of such researches, there appeared to be a good possibility that the full story of plant domestication might be unravelled not in New Mexico or in Tamaulipas but further to the south, in the heart of Mexico itself.

Fig. 11. Ovoid biface of obsidian and matting fragment, Archaic Period of Tamaulipas. 1/2

Fig. 10 (opposite). Characteristic chipped stone tools of the Tamaulipas Archaic. a–b, prismatic blades; c, small disk scraper; d, side scraper; e, split pebble chopper; f, flat scraping plane; g, gouge; h, pebble chopper. 1/2

Mexico

SANTA MARTA ROCK-SHELTER

As one travels west from the Grijalva Basin, the Chiapas highlands grow increasingly arid. Santa Marta rock-shelter lies in this dry zone, near the town of Ocozocoautla on the Pan American Highway, and was tested by MacNeish and Peterson in 1959. Five successive Archaic occupations in the cave were directly overlain by pottery-bearing deposits ascribable to the Early Formative horizon. Radiocarbon dates for the Archaic levels indicate a span from at least 6700 B C through an extremely dry post-Cochrane period (after 5000 B C). The complex of *cf. Fig. 9* tool and point types duplicates that of Tamaulipas, and includes Almagre, Nogales, and Abasolo points, gouges, scraper planes, pebble manos and boulder querns, etc. Four burials were found together, three of them flexed in foetal posture and one extended above, all of the dead having been covered as a group with metates. Burials of this sort occur in Desert Culture contexts as far north as Wyoming.

Maize pollen makes its appearance only in the Early Formative occupation, both pollens and other maize plant parts being completely absent from the pre-pottery levels. So, we might draw the conclusion that in the search for maize origins, Chiapas, on the south-eastern periphery of Mexico, is perhaps too far south, just as Tamaulipas appears to be too much to the north.

THE TEHUACÁN VALLEY

The most exciting news in Mexican archaeology in recent years has been the announcement that what appears to be the remains of wild maize had actually been discovered in archaeological deposits in highland Mexico. In 1960, MacNeish turned his attention to the Tehuacán Valley in south-eastern Puebla. Lying in the rain shadow of the mountains which protect it on the east, the valley is an arid cactus- and thorn-scrub-covered desert not unlike some parts of Arizona. MacNeish's preliminary reconnaissance of the bone-dry caves which border the valley led to a four-season project which uncovered, at long last, the remains of wild maize as well as the earliest cultivated variety.

It will be remembered that the Ajuereado phase, an Early Hunters occupation of the valley, ended about 6500 B C. During the succeeding

El Riego phase (*c.* 6500–4800 BC), two significant changes had come about. The first is that the climate turned warmer, perhaps resulting in the disappearance of 'big game'. The second is that by the end of the phase, the Tehuacán people had begun interfering with the evolution of certain plants: surely domesticated were the avocado, chili peppers, amaranth (this remained a grain crop of secondary importance right through the Spanish Conquest), and walnut squash. While population size increased, the people remained seasonally nomadic. Dry-season camps were occupied by tiny microbands, which coalesced into macrobands during the spring and wet season, when plant foods were more abundant. The concern with plant foods is reflected in the appearance of ground stone mortars and pestles, milling stones, and pebble manos.

There are some surprising features in El Riego. Two bolls of domestic cotton (*Gossypium hirsutum*) were recovered, apparently the world's first. Some quite elaborate burials from the phase were found in caves, the bodies being wrapped in blankets and nets, and the heads sometimes removed, ceremonially smashed, and deposited in baskets.

One of the great transition points in New World prehistory is to be seen in the Coxcatlán phase (*c.* 4800–3500 BC). The economy and settlement pattern remained much the same, But to the list of domesticates were added the bottle gourd, common bean, and warty squash – the evidence is now quite clear that these and other plants were domesticated in different places and at different times. But most important is the appearance of maize for the first time. This proved to be of two types, a wild variety and an early domesticated one which was probably planted when microbands came together in the spring. The miniscule cobs of wild maize so closely approach the reconstructed ancestor of maize in every respect, that Mangelsdorf is confident that the ancestor of corn has been found. In particular, they exhibit the extended glumes, the tiny kernel size, and the bearing of the male tassel on the ear of the hypothetical progenitor, as well as showing no variation among themselves, a wild characteristic. However, as recent proponents of the *teosinte* theory of maize origins have pointed out, they also look distressingly like *teosinte*! The revived controversy is yet to be decided.

Fig. 12

The succeeding Abejas phase (*c.* 3500–2300 BC) saw a distinct change in the Tehuacán settlement pattern, with small hamlets of five to

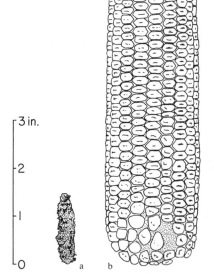

3 in.

2

1

0

a   b

Fig. 12. Comparison of ancient and modern maize. a, charred cob from Coxcatlán Cave, Puebla; b, modern dent corn

ten pithouses; probably none of these was occupied the year round. Domestic plants newly added to the cuisine were tepary beans (*Phaseolus acutifolius*), perhaps the pumpkin, and hybrid maize showing in-trogression ('capture' of genes by backcrossing) with *teosinte*. A study of Abejas coprolites made by the late Eric Callen reveals that 70 per cent of the diet was still based on wild plants and animals. It will be seen in the next chapter that Early Formative pottery centres on the neckless jar or *tecomate*, and the flat-bottomed bowl with outslanting sides; it is probably significant that in Abejas these same shapes are seen in beautifully made ground stone vessels, perhaps prototypes for later ceramics.

In fact, during the final Archaic phase in the valley, the poorly known Purrón (*c.* 2300–1500 BC), crude, gravel-tempered pottery is fashioned in the same shapes that are seen in the Abejas stone vessels. Similar ceramics have been found on the coast of Guerrero, and have coeval radiocarbon dates. Many archaeologists believe that the idea of pottery spread to Mexico from northern South America, where very ancient ceramics dating to the beginning of the third millennium BC have been found.

OTHER ARCHAIC SITES

Sporadic finds of cultural remains attributable to the Archaic period have been obtained at widely scattered sites in Mexico, but these hardly have the same scope or importance as the manifestations above outlined. Among these are some apparently pre-pottery levels in shell middens at Puerto Marquez and Islona de Chantuto on the Pacific coast and a series of hearths from an open site near Yanhuitlán, Oaxaca, and containing nothing but scrapers, choppers, and crude pebble manos. In the last few years, new excavations have added to the Archaic picture. In the Valley of Oaxaca, Kent Flannery and his associates have uncovered a long preceramic sequence paralleling that of Tehuacán, while on the Gulf Coast of Veracruz Jeffrey Wilkerson has a littoral version of the Archaic pattern. One of the most significant discoveries has been at Tlapacoya, once an isolated island in the southern part of the Valley of Mexico; circular houses like those of the Abejas phase have been uncovered, along with an extremely crude female figurine of pottery, dated 2300 BC ± 100, the oldest discovered in Mesoamerica and apparently the beginning of a tradition that was to flourish in the Formative.

THE ARCHAIC PERIOD AND THE ORIGINS OF SETTLED LIFE

The idea that the invention and adoption of food production led to a 'revolution' in the advancement of mankind was elaborated by the late V. Gordon Childe and has influenced the way of thinking of almost all who deal with this point in man's history. At the time that he wrote, almost nothing was known of the transition between the hunting and gathering and the food-producing way of life, either in the Old World or in the New. The mere absence of the evidence made the jump seem almost more sudden than recent work has shown it to have actually been. Now, for both Peru and Mexico, we have evidence of a very slow progress towards fully settled life: the alleged 'revolution' was seemingly more in the nature of a leisurely evolution. Yet, it cannot be denied that the consequences of food production were in the long run of the greatest import. Deevey has demonstrated that the density of population of peoples on the Neolithic (or Formative) level of food-getting is 25 times greater than the figure for primitive hunters and gatherers – the domestication of plants and animals obviously resulted in a quantum increase in the world's population, no matter how long the process took.

In Mexico, and probably in Mesoamerica in general, the development of plant cultivation took place during the Archaic period in a context which is almost indistinguishable from that of the Desert Culture, known so well in the Great Basin country of the American West. Back in this remote time, the ancestors of the mighty Aztecs and other civilised peoples of Mexico probably closely resembled the miserable 'Digger Indians' of Nevada and California, so despised by Mark Twain and other western travellers of the Victorian era. Semi-nomadic bands were forced into a seasonal cycle of hunting and collecting by the poverty of the rainless Mexican environment. As the Hypsithermal wore on, however, their efficiency at collecting plant foods began to outweigh their hunting prowess, with an increasing amount of settling down – seasonal camps took on the appearance of tiny villages. As the result of systematic exploitation of certain kinds of plants, especially of wild grasses like maize, vegetable foods and their energy were tamed and captured. According to present evidence, the process began with the bottle gourd, which may have been an accidental introduction, followed by pumpkins, beans, and chili peppers. Maize was most likely domesti-

Fig. 12

cated in central Mexico by the middle of the fifth millennium before Christ, although at that time it hardly resembled the giant hybrid plants of modern Iowa cornfields. Other domesticated food plants are much later and may even have been disseminated to Mexico from South America.

By the time of the first village-farming cultures, at the onset of the Formative, there were already present many of the features of settled life:

all of the important domesticates, the milling stones and manos on which maize was prepared, baskets, nets, cordage, mats, and apparently even wattle-and-daub houses. With the elaboration of pottery and with the yet mysterious improvement of maize at this great transition, the stage is set for a way of life that has remained unaltered to this day in the peaceful backwaters of Mexico.

CHAPTER IV

The Formative Period: Early Villagers

In the late nineteenth century, there was really no idea at all of the sequence of development in pre-Spanish Mexico. Of course, everyone knew perfectly well that the Aztecs were quite late, and there was a vague feeling that the great ruins of Teotihuacán were somehow the products of an earlier people, but that was about all. Imagine the delight, then, of Mexican antiquarians when there began to appear in their collections little, handmade, clay figurines, of a naïve and amusing style totally removed from that of the mould-made products of later peoples in the Valley of Mexico. Most astonishing was their obvious antiquity, for some had been recovered from deposits underlying the *Pedregal*, the lava covering much of the south-western part of the Valley. Scholars, prone to labels, immediately named the culture which had produced the figurines and the very abundant pottery associated with it 'Archaic', and in 1911 and 1912 Manuel Gamio demonstrated stratigraphically that the central Mexican sequence runs from earliest to latest: 'Archaic', Teotihuacán, Aztec.

cf. Plates 8, 9

It was not very long before the 'Archaic' or something like it was turning up all over Mexico and Central America, wherever, in fact, the archaeological spade went deep enough. Similar materials were found even in South America: in Peru, along the waterways of the Amazon basin, and on the Caribbean coast of Venezuela. On the basis of this distribution, Herbert J. Spinden in 1917 proposed that there was an 'Archaic' basement, so to speak, underlying all of the civilisations of the Western Hemisphere, a unitary culture which had originated with the supposed first domestication of maize in the Valley of Mexico and which had spread with that plant everywhere, bearing along the little figurines as a hall-mark. Quite naturally, this idea, which was based on incomplete and faulty evidence, met with very determined opposition, especially by those whose subsequent delvings into 'Archaic' remains had shown them the considerable diversity within this allegedly monolithic culture.

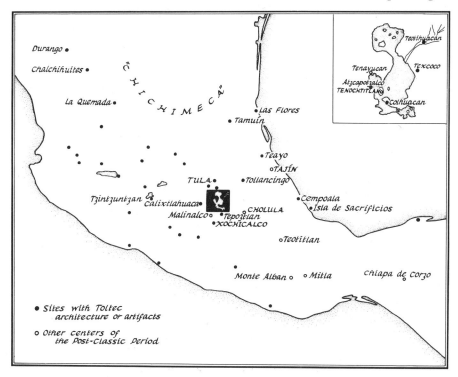

Fig. 13. Sites of the Formative Period. Shown in inset is the distribution of Formative centres in the Valley of Mexico

As will be seen, with the work of the last few decades we have returned full circle to the Spinden hypothesis. The Formative or Pre-Classic period, as the 'Archaic' is now known, was a time when Mesoamerica really was linked to the Andean Area – that as Spinden had so brilliantly guessed, the higher New World cultures do, in fact, rest on a single Formative base. But the details of this picture are quite different from those brushed on with so free a hand over fifty years ago!

Let us define the Formative as that epoch when farming based on maize, beans, and squash really became effective – effective in the sense that villages, and hamlets had sprung up everywhere in Mexico. As such, the Formative period is quite comparable to the Neolithic of the Old World, and almost all of the Neolithic arts, with the exception of animal husbandry, were present: the construction of compact settlements, pottery, loom weaving, working of stone by grinding as well as chipping, and the modelling of female figurines in clay.

Villages mean more people, and more people are, broadly speaking, the result of a greatly increased supply of food. What had happened to bring this about? As outlined in the previous chapter, the plants involved had already been domesticated for several millennia prior to the Formative. We may be seeing the result of a hasty improvement in the size and number of kernels of the maize ear through increased introgression of *teosinte.* A resulting population spiral of the most Malthusian sort could have suddenly filled all of Mexico with landhungry farmers, and camps and hamlets might have become permanently settled villages in almost a few generations.

When did this take place? Somewhat arbitrarily, it must be admitted, we set the lower limits of the Formative at the first appearance of pottery in abundance, about 1500 B C according to recent radiocarbon dates. The upper boundary is placed at the end of the third century of our era, at which point Teotihuacán civilisation was initiated and the Classic Maya began to carve their first dated monuments. Thus, these dates bracket a long, relatively tranquil span of some eighteen centuries.

It might also be reasonably asked why it took so long for the Mexicans to cross the threshold to villagefarming life. In the Old World this event first occurred, along the hilly flanks of Mesopotamia, as early as the seventh millennium before Christ, not very much later than the first experimentation with plant and animal domestication. In Mexico, where the American Indian originally took this step, the process of domestication took at least four and a half millennia; was this delay caused by the lack of domesticable animals, by the nature of the plants domesticated, by the cultural milieu of Mexico, or by some other factor? Whatever the answer, a handicap of this kind is the real reason why sixteenthcentury Mexico was the inferior of Europe, for once past the frontier into peasant life, ancient Mexican culture unfolded at the same rate as did that of the Old World. Given this late start, the civilisation that Cortés destroyed should be compared not to Renaissance Europe, but to the Bronze Age of the Near East and China.

Archaeologists are generally agreed that the Formative development can be divided into three parts: Early, from 1500 to 900 BC; Middle, from 900 to 300 BC; and Late, from 300 BC to before AD 300. It is also increasingly apparent, as we shall see, that both simple village cultures and advanced states can be detected in all three subperiods. The emerging picture is far more intricate than could have been imagined fifty or even twenty years ago.

VILLAGE CULTURES OF THE EARLY FORMATIVE

Knowledge of the Early Formative is relatively recent; in part this is the result of Mormon interest in Chiapa de Corzo, which archaeologists of the Church of Jesus Christ of the Latter Day Saints believe might have been one of the cities described in the Book of Mormon.

Excavations in that site, lying in the centre of the Grijalva Depression of Chiapas, have disclosed no less than eighteen successive occupations from the earliest times to the present. For much of its history, the Grijalva drainage basin seems to have been little more than a buffer state between the Maya to the east and an assortment of lesser nations to the west, south, and north. However, in the Formative period each of several distinctive cultures was linked to other more distant village and state cultures of south-eastern Mexico.

As reconstructed from debris recovered deep in a test pit, the Chiapa I, or Cotorra, phase presents us with the very beginnings of Formative life. A single radiocarbon date falls in the thirteenth century BC, but the total span of the culture is estimated to be about 1500 to 1000 BC. Admittedly we have only a fragmentary picture of the first farmers at Chiapa de Corzo, but they prepared their maize on simple milling stones which are heavily worn and thus must have been rare, and manufactured solid, handmade clay figurines. Their pottery was advanced in technique and quite sophisticated in form and decoration. Most of it consists of a hard, monochrome white or two-colour red-and-white ware, in the shape of dishes and large storage jars which might be either simple globular or else necked. Of some interest is the plastic decoration found on the rims of otherwise plain neckless jars: brushing with a handful of vegetable fibres, rows of gouges effected with the thumbnail, dimples popped out from the vessel interior, and plain rocker-stamping.

Fig. 14

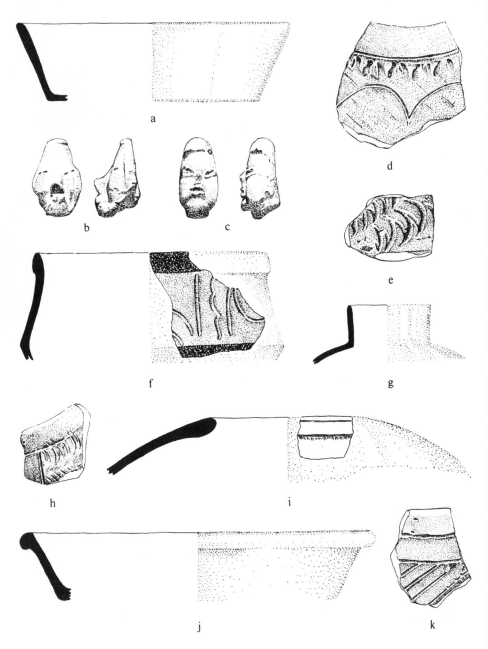

a

b

c

d

e

f

g

h

i

j

k

Now, rocker-stamping is a most peculiar way to alter the surface of a jar or dish. The trick is to 'walk' the edge of a crescentic implement held in the hand across the damp clay in such a way that curved, zig-zag patterns are produced. Rocker-stamping is found on pots of the allied and coeval Ocós culture of the Pacific coast of Guatemala, where the tool used was the crinkly edge of a cardium shell; and, in fact, the technique was known to Formative peoples all the way from the Valley of Mexico to Peru. Whatever its point of origin, rocker-stamping is thought to have spread through the advanced regions of the New World at a fairly early date.

Fig. 14, e, h

Vestiges of a culture much like Chiapa I lie just above the latest Archaic occupation of Santa Marta cave, further west in Chiapas (see Chapter III), and are accompanied by the pollen of maize and other plants indicating a very wet phase. Quite certainly, the farmers of the Early Formative enjoyed a climate which contrasted with the rainless conditions of the preceding Archaic.

THE SITE OF TLATILCO

The simple picture of a myriad of 'neolithic'-looking villages such as that at Chiapa de Corzo scattered over the Mexican countryside without any great social differentiation among them is an over-simplification. Evidence from excavations in the Valley of Mexico suggests that some settlements had already taken precedence over others in both social rank and in economic advantage. The key site for the Early Formative in the Valley is Tlatilco, which came to light in 1936 during excavations carried out by brickworkers digging for clay, not, alas, by archaeologists. The visitor to the site today will find nothing but a series of huge holes in the ground, surrounded by brick factories and slums. In actuality, only a tiny fraction of Tlatilco was ever cleared under scientific conditions.

Settled by about 1200 B C, Tlatilco was a very large village sprawling over about 160 acres. Located to the west of the great lake on a small

Fig. 14 (opposite). Early Formative ceramics, Chiapa I phase (1500–1000 B C), from Chiapa de Corzo. a, dish; b–c, figurine heads; d, e, h, i, k, rim fragments from neckless jars (e and h are rocker-stamped); g, fragment of necked jar; j, dish with thickened rim. a–f, h, j and k, 3/8; g and i, 3/16

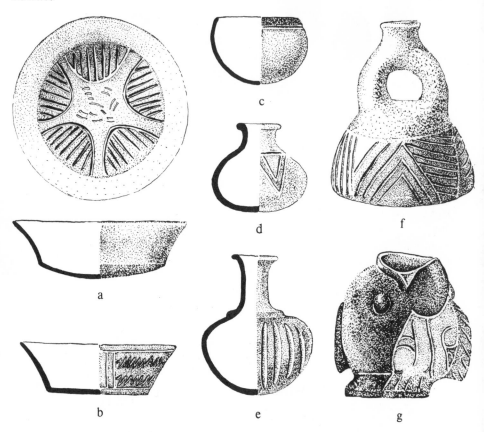

Fig. 15. Representative pottery vessels from Tlatilco, Early Formative Period. a, polished brown bowl with 'sunburst' striations on the interior; b, rocker-stamped dish; c, red-rimmed bowl; d–e, necked jars; f, black stirrup-spout jar; g, black effigy jar in the shape of a fish, polished in zones. 1/4

stream, it was not very far removed from the lakeshore where fishing and the snaring of birds could be pursued. In the Tlatilco refuse are the bones of deer and water-fowl, while represented in the potter's art are armadillo, opossum, wild turkey, bears, frogs, rabbits, fish, ducks, and turtles. Conspicuously present in those parts of the site actually excavated by archaeologists were the outlines of underground pits. Resembling in cross-section truncated cones, they were filled with dark earth, charcoal, ashes, figurine and pottery fragments, animal bones, and lumps of burned clay from the walls of pole-and-thatch houses; they must have served originally for the storage of grain belonging to various households.

No less than 340 burials were uncovered by archaeologists at Tlatilco, but there must have been many hundreds more destroyed by brick-workers (sometimes at the instigation of unscrupulous collectors). All of these were extended skeletons accompanied by the most lavish offerings, especially by figurines which only rarely appear as burial furniture in Formative Mexico.

There are two sorts of figurines: one that is large and hollow, and painted red, and the other small, solid, and of incredibly delicate and sophisticated workmanship. The latter usually represent girls with little more to wear than paint applied in patterns (probably with the clay roller stamps which have been found in the excavations), although some are attired in what would seem to be grass skirts. Here we encounter males as well, clothed in a simple breechclout. What an extraordinary glimpse of the life of these Formative aristocrats is provided in their figurines! We see women affectionately carrying children or dogs; dancers, some with rattles around the legs; acrobats and contortionists; and matrimonial couples on couches. While no courts are known for this period, it nevertheless is certain that the ball game was played, for one figurine shows a player with the protection for the hand and knee required by that sport.

A distinctly macabre streak appears in the art of the inhabitants of Tlatilco, possessed by a psychological bent that delighted in monstrosities. To illustrate this point, one might mention such representations as two-headed persons, or heads with three eyes, two noses and two mouths; hunchbacks; idiots; horribly ugly and sometimes masked individuals who may be shamans; and many other outrageous deformities. Several actual clay masks have been found, of the most sinister appearance; a few of these are oddly split vertically into two distinct faces, one of which might be a skull, for instance, and the other half an idiot with protruding tongue. Let it be noted here that dualism, the unity of basically opposed principles such as life and death, constitutes the very basis of the later religions of Mexico, no matter how great their complexity. Here we see the origin of the concept.

Fig. 16

Plates 8, 9

Mexico

Fig. 15

The pottery of Tlatilco bears a vague relation to the later peasant wares of El Arbolillo and Zacatenco, but there the resemblance ends. Within the bounds of the Formative tradition of plastic decoration and the restrained use of colour, the potters of this village made ceramics which are among the most aesthetically satisfying ever produced in ancient Mexico. Forms include bowls, neckless jars, long-necked bottles, little spouted trays (possibly for libations), bowls and jars with three tall feet, and, most peculiarly, jars with spouts which resemble stirrups. One or two colours of slip such as red and white are sometimes applied; colours and all kinds of roughening of the surface are confined to definite areas of the vessel by broad, grooved outlines. Particularly favoured were contrasting zones of matt and polished surfaces, as well as zoned rocker-

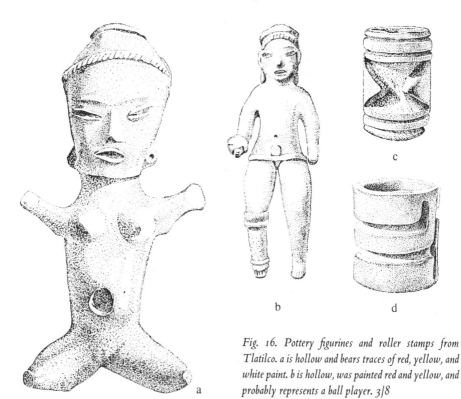

c

b   d

Fig. 16. Pottery figurines and roller stamps from Tlatilco. a is hollow and bears traces of red, yellow, and white paint. b is hollow, was painted red and yellow, and probably represents a ball player. 3/8

a

stamping. Designs such as stylised jaguar paws were carried out by cutting away part of the surface, the deep areas often filled with bright red pigment after firing.

There was great excitement in archaeological circles when the Tlatilco complex came to light, for something resembling it was already known elsewhere – thousands of miles to the south, in Peru. There also, in the very earliest civilisation of the South American continent, the Chavín culture (*c.* 1100–400 BC), were found such odd pottery shapes as stirrup-spouts and long-necked bottles, associated with unusual techniques like rocker-stamping and red-filled excising, as well as roller seals, figurines of Mexican appearance and split-face dualism. A chance resemblance or not? When two *complexes*, consisting of more than isolated traits, are so close, and manifestly coeval, it cannot be a matter of mere chance. Since this odd assortment quite suddenly appears at about 1000 BC on the north coast of Peru, along with an improved variety of maize, the only conclusion that can be drawn is that in some way or another, a group of Mexicans had travelled to the Andean area. But there is nothing like it in the intervening area, and it is considered likely that the journey (or journeys) was made by sea, perhaps via the great ocean-going rafts or huge dugout canoes which were heavily engaged in commerce along the Pacific coast when the Spaniards first arrived.

This all sounds very much like the Spinden hypothesis, which proposed a unified spread of Formative culture with maize and pottery, out of Mexico to the south, the harbinger of the civilisations which were to rise from this foundation. On the other hand, a crude sort of pottery, probably locally developed, and primitive maize which must have been diffused from Mexico in the second millennium BC were already in Peru before the critical epoch when the Tlatilco complex was introduced – so that while agreeing that the Formative cultures of the two great areas actually were intimately related to each other, and that the major flow of traits was from north to south, we must temper the hypothesis with the caution that the contact was extremely complicated and is not yet fully clarified.

No mention has yet been made of another curious element in the burial offerings of Tlatilco, namely, the very distinct presence of a strange art style known to have originated at the same time in the swampy jungles of the Gulf Coast. This style, called 'Olmec', was produced by the first civilisation of Mesoamerica, and its weird iconography which combined the lineaments of a snarling jaguar with that of a baby is unmistakably apparent in many of the figurines and in much of the pottery. The great expert on the pre-Spanish art of Mexico, Miguel Covarrubias, reasoned that the obviously greater wealth and social superiority of the Tlatilco people over their more simple contemporaries in the Valley of Mexico were the result of an influx of Olmec aristocrats from the eastern lowlands. This may possibly have been so, but it is equally likely that these villagers were a favourably placed people under heavy influence from 'missionaries' spreading the Olmec faith, without a necessary movement of populations. But more about the Olmecs in the next chapter.

ESTABLISHED VILLAGES OF THE MIDDLE FORMATIVE

Let us turn now from the incomplete data of the Early Formative to the wealth of information which is at hand for the villages girdling the Valley of Mexico during the middle range (*c.* 900–300 B C) of that period. A word of caution, however – because of our good knowledge of these sites, the impression has been given that the Valley had more ancient Formative beginnings than elsewhere. On the contrary, that isolated basin was probably a laggard in cultural development until the Classic period, when it became and stayed the flower of Mexican civilisation. Notwithstanding its later glory, the Valley was then a prosperous but provincial backwater, which occasionally received new items developed elsewhere.

These Middle Formative villages fringed the placid waters of the great lake, once more fully expanded. From the reed-covered marshes, abounding in waterfowl, across the rich, soft soils in the bottomlands of the Valley, to the forested hills populous with deer, this was an environment favourable in the extreme. Perhaps the surroundings were too bountiful for the stimulation that a people seem to need in order to make real progress: no challenge, and therefore no response, in the scheme of Professor Toynbee.

The first phase at the site of El Arbolillo seems to mark the initial Middle Formative occupation of the Valley. This little village was established directly on the sands of a beach fronting an arm of the great lake. Protected from the chill winds of winter by the slopes of a nearby hill, the farmers drew sustenance from the products of their fields and from the lake. That the village was occupied for many centuries is indicated by the more than 23 feet of accumulated midden deposits cut into by the excavator, consisting of refuse, casts of maize leaves, and burned daub fallen from the walls of pole-and-thatch huts.

Zacatenco, another site similarly placed on the edge of the lake, provides further evidence for the intensity of the village-farming life in the Valley. So much refuse was deposited in the Early Zacatenco phase (which follows on the heels of El Arbolillo I), that the villagers were forced to level it from time to time as terraces along which they built their wattle-and-daub houses.

Farmers they were, but the chase also provided much food to the Zacatenco and El Arbolillo peasants, as is well documented in the immense quantities of bones from deer and aquatic birds in their refuse. They hunted with small lance points chipped from obsidian, a hard, black volcanic glass worked with ease. Deer provided not only meat but also hides, which were cleaned of fat with little obsidian scrapers, and bones from which were fashioned awls and bodkins for working baskets and skins. Within each house, the farmer's wife ground the soaked maize on the familiar quern, although for some reason this was absent at El Arbolillo. For cooking and storage, they had a pleasant but undistinguished pottery, usually reddish-brown in colour and finely burnished; a somewhat better ware was produced at El Arbolillo, little three-legged bowls, smoked black, with red paint rubbed into geometric designs incised on the surface.

At these two sites and elsewhere in the Valley the midden deposits are literally stuffed with thousands of fragments of clay figurines, all female, providing a lively view of the costume of the day, or its lack. Although nudity was apparently the rule, these little ladies have elaborate face and body painting in black, white, and red; headdresses and coiffures as shown were very fancy, wrap-around turbans being most common. The technique of manufacture was about like that with which gingerbread men are made, features being indicated by a combination of punching and filleting. Significantly, no recognisable depictions of gods or goddesses have ever been identified in these villages, suggesting the possibility that the only cult was that of the figurines, which may have been objects of household devotion like the Roman *lares,* perhaps concerned with the fertility of the crops.

The dead were buried under the floors of houses, the usual fashion in Mesoamerica, but also occasionally together in cemeteries. With knees drawn up against the chest and wrapped in the mat upon which he had slept in life, the deceased was placed in a simple grave dug in the sand, although sometimes this was outlined and covered by stone slabs. A few pots or implements dropped in the grave, and a jade bead occasionally placed in the mouth (a symbol of life here and in China), tell something of a belief in an existence after death. Child mortality was high, as a good percentage of the skeletons found are of immature individuals.

LATE FORMATIVE CULTURES OF THE CENTRAL HIGHLANDS

The Olmec stimulus had been absent from the Valley of Mexico since 900 BC, and cultural development proceeded along its own lines. The isolation of the Valley from what was happening in the rest of Mesoamerica became even more pronounced in the period from 300 BC to AD 100. The mainstream of higher culture in that period was running through the lowlands of eastern Mexico and up the river valleys into the Southern Highlands and south-eastern part of the Republic, ignoring the Valley. This isolation holds true for much of the central highland region, except where direct Olmec intrusions had taken place.

Bright colours and an increase in the size and length of vessel feet were the concern of the potter in Late Formative times. The predilection towards the use of two or more colours in ceramic decoration is well illustrated by Chupícuaro, the burial ground of a village which lay above the Lerma River in the state of Guanajuato, about 80 miles north-west of the Valley of Mexico. While the Chupícuaro complex is widespread in the region, until recent excavations it was known, like Tlatilco, only from commercial pot-hunting. The skeletons of 390 individuals were found, almost all of whom had been laid on their backs in simple graves with abundant offerings of pottery, figurines, jade, and various clay objects. The later Mexicans believed that the owner's dog would help his soul across their equivalent of the Styx, and we find at Chupícuaro that dogs were also interred, many of them with great care.

Plate 10   The pottery vessels found in the cemetery are in both shape and decoration quite exuberant. In form one encounters bowls with all sorts of supports: short tripods, very long and attenuated tripods, swollen feet in the shape of breasts, pedestal bases. There are a few stirrup-spout jars, the last time this odd type is seen in Mexico, although it continued to enjoy great popularity in Peru until Colonial days. Vessel painting is lively, the slips used most often being red on buff, red and black on buff, or red and brown on buff, in finely proportioned, abstract designs which appear to have been derived from textiles. Little handmade, clay figurines of the 'pretty lady' type were likewise dropped into the graves; these are charming and quite nude, with slanting eyes and fancy coiffures built up from clay strips.

Plate 7

The most notable advance in the late Formative of central Mexico was the appearance of the temple-pyramid. The earliest temples of the highlands were thatch-roof, perishable structures not unlike the houses of the common people, erected within the community on low earthen platforms faced with sun-hardened clay. There are a few slight indications that some such platforms once existed at Tlatilco. By the Late Formative, however, they had become almost universal, as the nuclei of enlarged villages and even towns. Towards the end of the period, clay facings for the platforms were occasionally replaced by retaining-walls of undressed stones coated with a thick layer of stucco, and the substructures themselves had become greatly enlarged, some-times rising in several stages or tiers. Here we have, then, a definite progression from small villages of farmers with but household figurine cults, to hierarchical societies with priest-rulers who could call the populace to build and maintain sizeable religious establishments.

How grandiose some of these substructures were can be seen at Cuicuilco, located to the south of Mexico City near the National University, in an area covered by the *Pedregal* – a grim landscape of broken, soot-black lava with a sparse flora eking out its existence in rocky crevices. The principal feature of Cuicuilco is a round platform, 387 feet in diameter and rising in four inwardly sloping tiers to a present height of 75 feet. Two ramps placed on either side of the platform provide access to the summit, which was crowned at one time by a cone-like construction which brought the total height to about 90 feet. Faced with volcanic rocks, the interior of the surviving structure is filled with sand and rubble.

Plate 11

It is little wonder that Cuicuilco was once thought to be of hoary antiquity, for the main structure, excavated many years ago, is surrounded and partly covered by lava which had flowed down from Xitli volcano, looming on the western horizon above the Valley floor. Estimates varying anywhere from 8,500 to 30,000 years were made for the age of the flow by competent authorities. But this was in the pre-radiocarbon era, and long prior to Vaillant's careful work on the cultural stratigraphy of the Valley.

On the grounds of the associated ceramics and figurines, quantities of which are found beneath the *Pedregal*, Cuicuilco is clearly Late Formative, as confirmed by new C14 dates. The doom of Cuicuilco was set some time around AD 100, an end which must have been spectacular. The young Xitli first sent out dust and ashes which fell in quantity on the site, then the great eruptions themselves began, molten lava pouring out over the south-western margin of the Valley. All must have fled in panic from the region. Did the inhabitants have any premonitions of the final cataclysm? One might think so, for prominent among the remains of their culture are clay incense burners in the form of Xiuhtecuhtli, who was Fire God and lord of the volcanoes among the ancient Mexicans.

CHAPTER V

The Formative Period: Early Civilisations

BACKGROUND OF CIVILISED LIFE

The advance in the arts and technology that is implied by the word 'civilisation' is usually involved with the idea of urbanism. It is generally agreed, however, that not only in the New World but also in the Old many great civilisations completely lacked true cities. One learns to one's surprise that such were missing among the ancient Cambodians, the Mycenaeans, and the Egyptians until the 18th Dynasty, nor did the Classic Maya of the New World ever live in cities.

'By their works ye shall know them,' and archaeologists tend to judge cultures as civilisations by the presence of great public works and unified, evolved, monumental art styles. Life became organised under the direction of an élite class, usually strengthened by writing and other techniques of bureaucratic administration. Early civilisations were qualitatively different from the tribal cultures which preceded them, and with which in some cases they co-existed. The kind of art produced by them reveals the sort of compulsive force which held together these first civilised societies, namely, a state religion in which the political leaders were the intermediaries between gods and men. The monumental sculpture of these ancient peoples therefore tends to be loaded with religious symbolism, calculated to strike awe in the breast of the beholder.

The reader should not be surprised, then, to find that some of the civilisations which we are to describe were not urban at all. With a very few exceptions, most of the later cultures of Mesoamerica were organised around what might be called 'élite centres', architectural clusters in which lived the rulers and the priestly hierarchies, along with all their retainers, with the great mass of the people in hamlets and villages scattered through the countryside. Such a pattern could only have worked if the rulers could have called on the surrounding peasantry as corvée labour to build and maintain the temples and palaces, and for food to support the non-farming specialists, whether kings, priests, or artisans. Writing sprang up early to ensure the proper operation of this process, and in conjunction with an elaborate ritual and civic calendar became the basis of organised life, whether civic, religious, or economic. Furthermore, in these centres were held at regular intervals the markets in which all sorts of food and manufactures of hinterland and centre changed hands. This is the basic Mesoamerican pattern, established in the Formative, and persisting until Conquest times in many areas.

THE OLMEC CIVILISATION

cf. Plates 18, 19, 20

The most ancient Mexican civilisation is that called 'Olmec'. For many years, archaeologists had known about small jade sculptures and other objects in a distinct and powerful style that emphasised human infants with snarling, jaguar-like features. Most of these could be traced to the sweltering Gulf Coast plain, the region of southern Veracruz and neighbouring Tabasco, just west of the Maya area. George Vaillant recognised the fundamental unity of all these works, and assigned them to the 'Olmecs', the mysterious 'rubber people' described by Sahagún as inhabiting jungle country of the Gulf Coast; thus the name became established.

Actually, nothing is known of the real people who produced Olmec art, neither the name that they called themselves by nor from where they came. Old poems in Náhuatl, recorded after the Conquest, speak of a legendary land called Tamoanchán, on the eastern sea, settled long before the founding of Teotihuacán

> *in a certain era*
> *which no one can reckon*
> *which no one can remember,*

where

> *there was a government for a long time.*[1]

Fig. 3

This tradition is intriguing, for Tamoanchán is not a good Náhuatl name but Maya, meaning 'Land of Rain or Mist'. It will be recalled that an isolated Maya language, Huastec, is still spoken in northern Veracruz. Linguists believe that before the time of Christ, there was an unbroken band of Maya speech extending along the Gulf Coast all the way from the Maya area proper to the Huasteca, and that the region in which the Olmec civilisation was established could have been in those distant times Maya-speaking. All this suggests that the Olmec homeland was the real Tamoanchán, and that the original 'Olmecs' spoke the Maya tongue.

There has been much controversy about the dating of the Olmec civilisation. The great Mexican scholars Alfonso Caso and Miguel Covarrubias held for a placement in the Formative period, largely on the grounds that Olmec traits have appeared in sites of that period in the Valley of Mexico. This position was strongly attacked by most North American archaeologists, who felt that a civilisation so advanced could be no earlier than the Classic (AD 300–900). Time has fully borne out the Mexican school. A long series of radiocarbon dates from the important Olmec site of La Venta span the centuries from 900 to 400 BC, placing the major development of this centre entirely within the Middle Formative. Another set of dates shows that the site of San Lorenzo is even older, falling within the Early Formative (1200 to 900 BC), making it contemporary with Tlatilco and other highland sites in which influence from San Lorenzo can be detected. There is now not the slightest doubt that all later civilisations in Mesoamerica, whether Mexican or Maya, ultimately rest on an Olmec base.

Fig. 17

The hallmark of Olmec civilisation is the art style. Its most unusual aspect is the iconography on which it is based, through which we glimpse a religion of the strangest sort. The Olmec evidently believed that at some distant time in the past, a woman had cohabited with a jaguar, this union giving rise to a race of were-jaguars, combining the lineaments of felines and men. These monsters are usually shown in Olmec art as somewhat infantile throughout life, with the puffy features of small, fat babies, snarling mouths, toothless gums or long, curved fangs, and even claws. The heads are cleft at the top, perhaps representing some congenital abnormality like *spina bifida*. Were-jaguars are always quite sexless, with the obesity of eunuchs. In one way or another, the concept of the were-jaguar is at the heart of the Olmec civilisation. What were these creatures in function?

A recent study by David Joralemon has convincingly shown that the Olmec worshipped a variety of deities, some of which can be recognised in the pantheons of much later peoples such as the Aztec. This disposes of a hypothesis once championed by Covarrubias in which only various guises of the Rain God are apparent.

Given its odd content, Olmec art is nevertheless 'realistic' and shows a great mastery of form. On the great basalt monuments of the Olmec 'heartland' and in other sculptures, scenes which include what are cf. Plate 22 apparently portraits of real persons are present; many of these are bearded, some with aquiline features. Olmec bas-reliefs are notable in the use of empty space in compositions. The combination of tension in space and the slow rhythm of the lines, which are always curved, produces the overwhelmingly monumental character of the style, no matter how small the object.

The Olmec were above all carvers of stone, from the really gigantic Colossal Heads, stelae, and altars of the Veracruz-Tabasco region, to finely carved jade celts, figurines, and pendants. Typical is a com- bination of carving, drilling (using a reed and wet sand), and delicate incising. Olmec sculptures are usually three-dimensional, to be seen from all sides, not just from the front. Very small sculptures and figurines of a beautiful blue-green jade and of serpentine were, of course, portable, so that we are not always sure of the place of origin of many of these pieces. Olmec objects of small size have been found all over Mexico, especially in the state of Guerrero in the western part of the Republic, but most of these could have been carried thence by aboriginal trade or even Plate 19 by Olmec missionaries. Among these are magnificent effigy axes of jade, basalt, or other stone, some of which are so thin and completely useless as axes that they must have had a ritual purpose. The ubiquitous were- jaguar is on all of these, sometimes inclining towards the feline, sometimes more anthropomorphic. The Olmec style was also repre- Plate 21 sented in pottery bowls and figurines, and even in wood (in a miraculously preserved mask with jade incrustations from a cave in Guerrero).

Fig. 13 The region of southern Veracruz and neighbouring Tabasco has been justifiably called the Olmec 'heartland'. Here is where the great Olmec sites and Olmec monuments are concentrated, and here is where the myth represented in Olmec art appears in its most elaborate form. There is hardly any question that the civilisation had its roots and its highest development in that zone, which is little more than 125 miles long by about 50 miles wide. The 'heartland' is characterised by a very high annual rainfall (about 120 inches) and, before the advent of the white man, by a very high, tropical forest cover. Much of it is swampy lowland, formed by the many rivers which meet the Gulf of Mexico near by. One might think that this inhospitable environment is an unlikely one to have produced the New World's first civilisation.

Discovered by Matthew Stirling in 1945 and excavated by Yale University from 1966 to 1968, the great Olmec site of San Lorenzo is located near the flat bottoms of the Coatzacoalcos River. The 150-foot-high plateau on which it is placed turned out to be partly man-made, with long ridges jutting out on its north-west, west, and south sides. San Lorenzo had first been settled about 1500 B C, but by 1200 B C had become thoroughly Olmec. At its height, some of the most magnificent and awe-inspiring sculptures ever discovered in Mexico were fashioned without the benefit of stone tools, from basalt which had been quarried in the Tuxtla Mountains, a straight-line distance of 50 miles. Presumably the stones were transported on great balsa rafts, first down to the coast of the Gulf of Mexico, then up the Coatzacoalcos River. The amount of labour which must have been involved staggers the imagination.

The Early Formative sculptures of San Lorenzo include seven Colossal Heads of great distinction. These are up to 9 feet 4 inches in height and weigh many tons; it is believed that they are portraits of mighty Olmec rulers, with heavy, thick-lipped, rather 'Negroid' features. They wear headgear rather like American football helmets, and it is likely that they served as protection for the ceremonial game played with a rubber ball throughout Mesoamerica. Also typical are the so-called 'altars': large basalt blocks with flat tops. On one side is usually sculptured a human figure seated in a niche. One of San Lorenzo's finest 'altars' was found near the satellite site of Potrero Nuevo, and depicts two pot-bellied, atlantean dwarfs supporting the 'altar' top with their upraised hands.

Plates 12, 13

Plate 14

We have discovered a great deal about the economic basis of early Olmec civilisation along the middle Coatzacoalcos. The bulk of the people were maize farmers, raising two crops a year on the more upland soils. In contrast, the Olmec élite had seized the rich river levees for themselves, where bumper crops are secured during the dry season after the rainy season floods have subsided. Hunting was of little importance, and certainly took second place to fish and human captives as a source of animal protein, according to the testimony of kitchen debris.

The rise of the first Mesoamerican state, dominated by a hereditary élite class with judicial and military power, seems to have been the result of two factors: first, an environment with very high agricultural potential due to year-round rains and wet-season inundations of the river margins, and second, differential access to the best of these lands by crystallising social groups. There was nothing egalitarian about San Lorenzo society. The nature of the controls and compulsion required to build the plateau and transport the monuments eventually led to a mighty cataclysm. About 900 BC San Lorenzo was destroyed either by invasion or revolution, or a combination of these. The grandiose monuments glorifying its rulers were ruthlessly smashed and defaced, then ritually buried in long lines within the ridges, never to be seen again until the coming of the archaeologist with pick and spade.

After the downfall of San Lorenzo, its power passed to La Venta, Tabasco, perhaps the greatest of all Olmec sites although now largely demolished by oil operations. It is located on an island in a sea-level coastal swamp near the Tonalá River, about 18 miles inland from the Gulf. The island has slightly more than two square miles of dry land. The site itself is in the northern half, and is a linear complex of clay

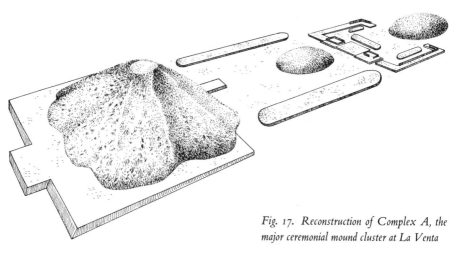

Fig. 17. Reconstruction of Complex A, the major ceremonial mound cluster at La Venta

constructions stretched out for $1\frac{1}{2}$ miles in a north–south direction; it has been extensively excavated, before its desecration by air strips, bulldozers, and parking lots, first by Matthew Stirling of the Smithsonian Institution and later by the University of California. The major feature at La Venta is a huge, volcano-shaped, pyramid of clay, 110 feet high. The idea behind such enormous mounds is of interest here, for this is the largest of its period in Mexico. It is almost as though man were struggling to get closer to the gods, to raise his temples to the sky. This cannot have been their only function, however, for inside many Mesoamerican pyramids have been found elaborate tombs, made during construction of the pyramids themselves, so that it is likely that the temple-pyramid was an outgrowth of the ancient idea of a burial mound or funerary monument. Whether this is so in the case of the La Venta pyramid we do not know, for although still extant it has never been penetrated.

Fig. 17

To the north of the Great Pyramid are two long, low mounds on either side of the centre-line, and a low mound in the centre between these. Then, one comes to a broad, rectangular court or plaza which was once surrounded by a fence of basalt columns, each about 7 feet tall, set side by side in the top of a low wall made of adobe bricks. Finally, along the centre-line, is a large, terraced clay mound. There are some who believe that the layout of the main portion of the site represents a gigantic, abstract jaguar mask.

Robert Heizer calculates that this élite centre must have been supported by a hinterland population of at least 18,000 persons; the main pyramid alone probably took some 800,000 man-days to construct. The nearest arable land is a 350-square-mile territory between the Coatza-coalcos and Tonalá Rivers, and it was perhaps on this that the rulers of La Venta depended for food and labour.

In its hey-day, the site must have been vastly impressive, for different coloured clays were used for floors, and the sides of platforms were painted in solid colours of red, yellow, and purple. Scattered in the plazas fronting these rainbow-hued structures were a large number of monuments sculptured from basalt. Outstanding among these are the Colossal Heads, of which four were found at La Venta. Large stelae (tall, flat monuments) of the same material were also present. Particularly outstanding is Stela 3, dubbed 'Uncle Sam' by archaeologists. On it, two elaborately garbed men face each other, both wearing fantastic headdresses. The figure on the right has a long, aquiline nose and a goatee. Over the two float chubby were-jaguars brandishing war clubs. Also typical are the so-called 'altars'. The finest is Altar 5, on which the central figure emerges from the niche holding a jaguar-baby in his arms; on the sides, four subsidiary adult figures hold other little were-jaguars, who are squalling and gesticulating in a lively manner. As usual, their heads are cleft, and mouths drawn down in the Olmec snarl.

Plate 15

A number of buried offerings, perhaps dedicatory, were encountered by the excavators at the site. These usually include quantities of jade or serpentine celts laid carefully in rows; many of these were finely incised with were-jaguar and other figures. A particularly spectacular offering comprised a group of 6 celts and 16 standing figurines of serpentine and jade arranged upright in a sort of scene. In some offerings were found finely polished ear flares of jade with attached jade pendants in the outline of jaguar teeth. Certain Olmec sculptures and figurines show persons wearing pectorals of concave shape around the neck, and such have actually come to light in offerings. These oddly enough turned out to be concave mirrors of magnetite and ilmenite, the reflecting surfaces polished to optical specifications. What were they used for? Experiments have shown that they can not only start fires, but also throw images on flat surfaces like a *camera lucida*. They were pierced for suspension, and one can imagine the hocus-pocus which some mighty Olmec priest was able to perform with one of these.

Plate 18

Three rectangular pavements, each about 15 feet by 20 feet, are known at La Venta. Each consists of about 485 blocks of serpentine, laid out in the form of a highly abstract jaguar mask. Certain details were left open and emphasised by filling with coloured clays. Strange as it may seem, these were also offerings, as they were covered up with many feet of clay and adobe layers soon after construction.

Plate 16

In the acid soil of La Venta, bones disappear quickly, and very few burials have been discovered. Of those found, however, the most outstanding was the tomb in Mound A-2, surrounded and roofed with basalt columns. On a floor made of flat limestone slabs were laid the remains of two juveniles, badly rotted when discovered, each wrapped up in a bundle and heavily coated with vermilion paint. With them had been placed an offering of fine jade figurines, beads, a jade pendant in the

Plate 17

shape of a clam shell, a sting-ray spine of the same substance, and other objects. Outside the tomb a sandstone 'sarcophagus' with a cover had been left, but other than some jade objects on the bottom, nothing was found within but clay fill. It could be that the children or infants in the tomb were monstrosities who to the Olmecs may have resembled were-jaguars and thus merited such treatment.

There is not much household debris on La Venta island. What little has been found, mainly away from the centre itself, consists of pottery and clay figurines of typically Middle Formative appearance. The shapes are largely flat-bottomed dishes and bowls; rocker-stamping is also present. The figurines, which are handmade, are preponderantly female with rather Olmec features, but some represent bearded males. Pottery roller stamps and prismatic blades of obsidian are also present.

La Venta was deliberately destroyed in ancient times. Its fall was certainly violent, as 24 out of 40 sculptured monuments were intentionally mutilated. This probably occurred in the beginning of Late Formative times, around 400–300 BC, for subsequently, following its abandonment as a centre, offerings were made with pottery of Late Formative cast. As a matter of fact, La Venta may never have lost its significance as a cult centre, for among the very latest caches found was a Spanish olive jar of the early Colonial period, and Professor Heizer suspects that offerings may have been made in modern times as well.

In its day, La Venta was undoubtedly the most powerful and holy place in the Olmec 'heartland', sacred because of its very inaccessibility, but other great Olmec centres also flourished in the Middle Formative. About 100 miles north-west of La Venta lies Tres Zapotes, in a setting of low hills above the swampy basin formed by the Papaloapan and San Juan Rivers. It comprises about 50 earthen mounds stretched out along the bank of a stream for two miles. Pottery and clay figurines recovered from stratigraphic excavations have revealed an early occupation of Tres Zapotes which was contemporaneous with La Venta, and a later occupation which post-dated the fall of that great centre. Belonging to this earlier, purely Olmec, horizon is a Colossal Head like those of La Venta. But the importance of Tres Zapotes lies in its famous stela, discussed below.

Thus far we have said nothing about writing and the calendar in the Olmec 'heartland'. Actually, no inscriptions or written dates have come to light at La Venta itself. None the less, a number of fine jade objects in the Olmec style, now in public and private collections but of unknown provenance, are incised with hieroglyphs. Although unreadable to us, some of them appear to be ancestral to certain Maya glyphs. If they can be assigned to the Middle Formative horizon, and there seems to be no valid reason not to consider them of that age, then these inscriptions mark the very beginnings of writing in Mexico.

It has already been said that Tres Zapotes survived into the Late Formative, after La Venta had been overthrown. Tres Zapotes has *Fig. 18* produced the oldest dated monument of the New World, Stela C, a fragmentary basalt monument which had been re-used in later times. On one side is a very abstract were-jaguar mask in a style which is *derivative* from Olmec, but not in the true canon. The reverse side bears a date in the Long Count.

Fig. 18. Long Count date on Stela C, Tres Zapotes

The Long Count system of calculating dates needs some explanation. In Chapter I, it was mentioned that all the Mesoamerican peoples had a calendar which entailed the meshing of the days of a 260-day 'Almanac Year' with those of the 365-day solar year. A day in one would not meet a day in the other for 52 years; consequently, any date could be placed within a single 52-year cycle by this means. This is the Calendar Round system, but it obviously is not much help when more than 52 years is involved, any more than a Maori would know what revolution occurred in '76, or a Choctaw what happened to an English king in '88, for it would require special knowledge to know in which century the event happened. A more exact way of expressing dates would be a system which counted days elapsed from a definite starting point, such as the founding of Rome or the birth of Christ. This is the role that was fulfilled by the Long Count, confined to the lowland peoples of Mesoamerica and taken to its greatest refinement by the Classic Maya. For reasons unknown to us, the starting date was 3113 BC, and dates are presented in terms of the numbers of periods of varying length which have elapsed since the mechanism was set in motion. For instance, the largest period was one of 144,000 days, the next of 7,200 days, then 360 days, followed by 20 days and one day. Coefficients were expressed in terms of bar-and-dot numerals, the bars having the value of five and the dots, one. Thus, a bar and two dots stand for 'seven'.

In Stela C, the coefficient accompanying the great first period was missing when the stone was discovered by Matthew Stirling, but he reconstructed it as seven. He read the entire date as (7).16.6.16.18, or 31 BC in terms of our calendar, raising a storm of protests from Mayanists who felt sure that a monument outside Maya territory could not be this old. Stirling was vindicated in 1969 when a Tres Zapotes farmer accidentally turned up the missing top part of the stela, complete with its coefficient of seven. Another date, this time with a fairly long, unread text, is inscribed on a small jade figure in epi-Olmec style, a duck-billed, winged figure with human features. This is the Tuxtla Statuette, discovered many years ago in the Olmec area, with the Long Count date of 8.6.2.4.17 (AD 162). Since both dates fall in the Late Formative and were found within the Olmec 'heartland', it is not unlikely that Olmec literati invented the Long Count and perhaps also developed certain astronomical observations with which the Maya are usually credited.

Fig. 19

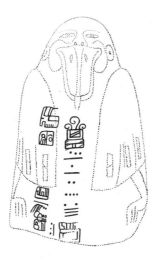

Fig. 19. The Tuxtla Statuette, with Long Count date and other hieroglyphs (after Holmes). Height 6 in.

Notwithstanding their intellectual and artistic achievements, the Olmec were by no means a peaceful people. Their monuments show that they fought battles with war clubs, and some individuals carry what seems to be a kind of cestus or knuckle-duster. Armed groups of Olmec warriors apparently invaded the Mexican plateau during the Middle Formative, for we have an isolated site of pure Olmec character at Chalcatzingo, Morelos, just south of the Valley of Mexico, where a bas-relief on a boulder shows three Olmec warriors brandishing clubs above an ithyphallic captive. Olmec objects are scattered in Middle Formative sites throughout the region. Down through Chiapas they went, along the Pacific coastal plain of Guatemala, leaving their monuments as far south as Chalchuapa, El Salvador, around 500 miles from their homeland, where a boulder is carved with warlike figures in their characteristic style. Perhaps these groups paved the way for missionaries who spread the cult of the Olmec jaguar god.

MONTE ALBAN I CIVILISATION

A high culture very reminiscent of that possessed by the Olmecs and quite conceivably derivative from it, arose in the Valley of Oaxaca in southern Mexico during Middle and Late Formative times. Its most important site is Monte Albán, constructed on a series of eminences about 1,300 feet above the floor of the valley. Monte Albán lies in the heart of the region still occupied by the Zapotec peoples; since there is no evidence for any major disruption in central Oaxaca until the beginning of the Post-Classic, about A D 900, archaeologists feel reasonably certain that the inhabitants of the site were always speakers of that language.

Most of the constructions that meet the eye at Monte Albán are of the Classic period. However, in the south-western corner of the site, which is laid out on a north–south axis, excavations have disclosed the Temple of the *Danzantes*, a stone-faced platform contemporary with the first occupation of the region, Monte Albán I. The so-called *Danzantes* (i.e. 'dancers') are bas-relief figures on large stone slabs set into the outside of the platform. Nude men with slightly Olmecoid features (i.e. the down-turned mouth), the *Danzantes* are shown in strange, rubbery postures as though they were swimming or dancing in a viscous fluid. Some are represented as old, bearded individuals with toothless gums or with only a single protuberant incisor. Over 140 of these strange yet powerful figures are known at Monte Albán, and it might be reasonably asked exactly what their function might be, or what they depict. The distorted pose of the limbs, the open mouth and closed eyes indicate that these are corpses, undoubtedly chiefs or kings slain by the earliest rulers of Monte Albán. In many individuals the genitals are clearly delineated, usually the stigma laid on captives in Mesoamerica where nudity was considered scandalous. Furthermore, there are cases of sexual mutilation depicted on some *Danzantes*, blood streaming in flowery patterns from the severed part. To corroborate such violence, one *Danzante* is nothing more than a severed head.

Plates 23, 24

Where we have little evidence for writing and the calendar in the Olmec area, there is abundant testimony of both these in Monte Albán I, whence come our first true literary texts in Mexico. These are carved in low relief on the *Danzantes* themselves and on other slabs. Numbers were symbolised by bars and dots, although a finger could substitute for a dot in the numbers 1 and 2. Caso has deduced that the glyphs for the days of the 260-day Almanac Year (based on a permutation of 20 named days with 13 numbers) were in use, as well as those for the 'months' of the solar year. Thus, these ancient people already had the 52-year cycle, the Calendar Round. However, the Long Count was seemingly not in

Fig. 20

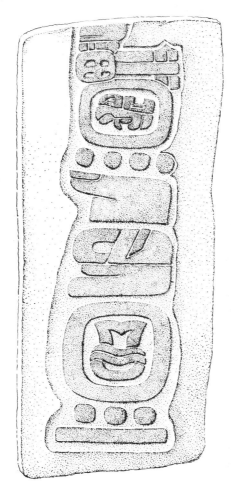

Fig. 20. Hieroglyphic inscription on large stone slab, Monte Albán. Monte Albán I culture (Formative Period)

use. A fair number of other hieroglyphs, unaccompanied by numerals, also occur, and these probably were symbols in a script which had both phonetic and ideographic elements, often combined (as in Chinese); some are so placed on the *Danzante* monuments as to attest to their function as proper names, but none can be read.

The pottery of Monte Albán I is known from tombs at this site and in others affiliated with it, such as Monte Negro. It is of a fine grey clay, a characteristic maintained throughout much of the development of Monte Albán. The usual shapes are vases with bridged spouts and bowls with large, hollow tripod supports – typical of the end of the Middle Formative and most of Late Formative. Probably the phase does not begin until about 500 BC and ends a few centuries after the time of Christ. Some of the vessels bear modelled and incised figures like the *Danzantes*, confirming the association.

Plate 26

The development from the first phase to Monte Albán II, which is Proto-Classic and therefore around AD 300, was peaceful and gradual. In the southernmost plaza of the site was erected Building J, a stone-faced construction in the form of a great arrowhead pointing south-west. Within it is a complex of dark, narrow chambers which have been roofed over by leaning together stone slabs to meet at the apex. The exterior of the building is set with a great many inscribed stone slabs all

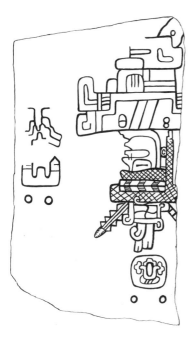

Fig. 21. Hieroglyphs representing a conquered town, from Building J at Monte Albán. Monte Albán II culture, Proto-Classic Period

Fig. 21

bearing a very similar text. These Monte Albán II inscriptions generally consist of an upside-down head with closed eyes and elaborate headdress, below a glyph for 'mountain' or 'town'; over this is the name of the place, seemingly given phonetically in rebus fashion (like the 'I saw Aunt Rose' puzzles of youth). In its most complete form, it is accompanied by the symbols for year, month and day, as well as various untranslatable glyphs. Such inscriptions are interpreted by Alfonso Caso as records of town conquests, the inverted heads being the defeated kings. It is possible that all are in the Zapotec language, but a phonetic reading has never been given.

This obsession with the recording of victories over enemies is one characterising early civilisations the world over, and the Formative cultures of Mexico were no exception. It speaks for a time when states were tiny and engaged in mutual warfare, when no ruler could consolidate his sway over more than a small territory.

IZAPAN CIVILISATION

The final culture of the Formative period upon which we will touch has never been investigated in the detail which it demands, for it is of high significance. This is the civilisation centred on the site of Izapa, located in the south-eastern part of the state of Chiapas on a tributary stream of the Suchiate River, which divides Mexico from Guatemala. We are here in the broad, Pacific coast plain, one of the most unbearably hot, but at the same time incredibly fertile, regions of Mexico. Izapa is a very large site, with numbers of earthen mounds faced with river cobbles, all forming a maze of courts and plazas in which the stone monuments are located. There is possibly a ball court, formed by two long, earth embankments. Samples of pottery taken from Izapa show it to be a Late Formative centre, persisting into the Proto-Classic Period.

The art style as expressed in bas-reliefs is highly distinctive. Although obviously derived from the Olmec, it differs from it in its use of large, cluttered, baroque compositions and anecdotal scenes with groups of people. This style appears on stone stelae which often are associated with 'altars' placed in front, the latter crudely carved to represent giant toads, symbols of rain. The principal god is a metamorphosis of the old were-jaguar (i.e. rain god) of the Olmecs, the upper lip now tremendously extended to the degree that it resembles the trunk of a tapir. Most scenes on Izapan stelae take place under a sky band in the form of stylised monster teeth, from which may descend a winged figure on a background of swirling clouds. On Stela 1, the 'Long-lipped God' is depicted with feet in the form of reptile heads, walking on water from which he dips fish to be placed in a basketry creel on his back, while on Stela 3, he brandishes a club above an elaborate serpent. Most interesting of all is Stela 21, on which a warrior holds the head of a decapitated enemy; in the background, an important person is carried in a sedan chair, the roof of which is embellished with a crouching jaguar.

Plate 25

The real importance of the Izapan civilisation is that it is the connecting link in time and space between the earlier Olmec civilisation and the later Classic Maya. Izapan monuments are found scattered down the Pacific coast of Guatemala and up into the highlands in the vicinity of Guatemala City. On the other side of the highlands, in the lowland jungle of northern Guatemala, the very earliest Maya monuments appear to be derived from Izapan prototypes. Moreover, not only the stela-and-altar complex, the 'Long-lipped God' (who becomes the Maya Long-nosed God), and the baroque style itself were adopted from the Izapan culture by the Maya, but the priority of Izapa in the very important adoption of the Long Count is quite clear-cut: the most ancient dated Maya monument reads A D 292, while a stela in Izapan style at El Baúl, Guatemala, bears a Long Count date 256 years earlier.

CHAPTER VI

The Classic Period

RISE OF THE GREAT CIVILISATIONS

By any criteria, the period from A D 300 to 900 was the most remarkable in the whole development of Mesoamerica. This era of florescence is the Classic, and it is at this time that the peoples of Mexico built civilisations that can bear comparison with those of other parts of the globe. With justification, the Classic is thought of as the Golden Age of Mexico, when the arts and sciences reached their highest refinement, when the seeds that were planted during the Formative reached their fruition.

Fig. 22

Literacy was now pan-Mexican, with the possible exception of the western regions. Although no books have survived into our day, we have every reason to believe that most peoples possessed them. Dates were recorded in terms of the 52-year Calendar Round, and in the lowlands the Long Count was used. What for, if not to write their own history?

From their genesis in the Olmec period the gods of Mexico had finally revealed themselves in all their bewildering variety. There had now crystallised a complete pantheon, one that was shared by all Mexicans. The most ubiquitous of these deities were the Rain God, metamorphosed from one of the Olmec were-jaguars; his consort, the Water Goddess; the Sun God; the Moon Goddess; and, most significantly, the Feathered Serpent, known to the later Nahuas as Quetzalcóatl. The latter was a culture hero, revered for his introduction of learning and art, and was considered the very essence of life on this earth.

Notably missing from this pantheon are the fierce war gods of the Post-Classic period, such as the Toltec Tezcatlipoca and the Aztec Huitzilopochtli, who had to be fed with the hearts of numberless sacrificial victims for their well-being. Quite the contrary: the recorded myths of the Quetzalcóatl cycle stress that he demanded sacrifice only of butterflies and snakes, not of humans. Coupled with this, there is little evidence for an obsession with warfare in Classic art, at least on the scale that the Toltecs and Aztecs practised it, and there is a general lack of

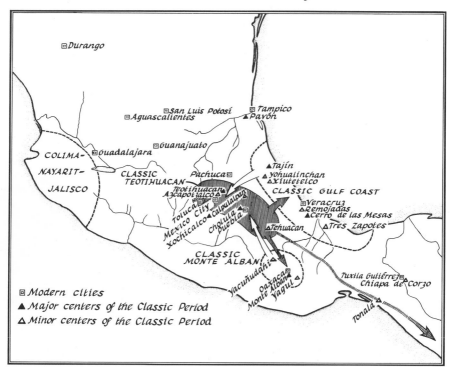

Fig. 22. Distribution of Classic Period sites. The shading indicates the area covered by the Classic Teotihuacán civilisation and its extensions in Mexico

fortifications. These conditions of relative peace are reflected in the art styles of the Classic, which are characterised by an untroubled serenity and sophistication, far removed from the tough and fearful productions of later times. Be that as it may, there has never been a people who did not indulge in warfare. In this connection the sudden spread of the art styles and products of some Classic civilisations has quite justly been interpreted as the result of conquest. Furthermore, in at least one area, the Gulf Coast, human sacrifice was probably not uncommon.

There must also have been many more people in Mexico during the Classic than formerly. Ruins are everywhere in the Republic, and most

87

are Classic. On the basis of a technology that was essentially Neolithic, for metals were unknown until after AD 900, the Mexicans raised fantastic numbers of buildings, decorated them with beautiful frescoes, produced pottery and figurines in unbelievable quantity, and covered everything with sculptures. Even mass production was introduced, with the invention (or importation from South America) of the clay mould for making figurines and incense burners. Behind this abundance was the same economic theme that had been emphasised by their prede-cessors: simple farming of maize, beans, and squash, reflected in the continued importance of nature gods in their pantheon. Some authors have claimed that the Classic achievement could only have resulted from utilisation of some form of irrigation, but for this there has never been found the slightest evidence.

Very clearly, the Classic florescence saw the intensification of sharp social cleavages throughout Mexico, and the consolidation of élite classes. It has long been assumed that the mode of government was theocratic, with a priestly group exercising temporal power. In lieu of actual documents from the period, there is little for or against this idea to be gained from the archaeological record. At any rate, below the intellectual group which held the political reins was a peasantry which had hardly changed an iota from Formative times. In fact, the old village-farming way of life has never, since its inception, been altered in any way until today.

How extensive was the sway of each state over surrounding territory may never be known; probably the élite centre type of site held less land and directed fewer people than the great urban state which then had its capital in the Valley of Mexico. In the case of the latter, we may be in the presence of an entity as large as, or larger than the famous Aztec empire of later days.

THE URBAN CIVILISATION OF TEOTIHUACÁN

True cities were rare anywhere in the Mesoamerican Classic, especially in Mexico. Of the few that did exist, the greatest of all was ancient Teotihuacán, the most important site in all Mexico – even Moctezuma II himself made frequent pilgrimages on foot to its ruins during late Aztec times. Memories of its greatness persisted in Náhuatl myths recorded after the Conquest, for it was then thought that the civilisation that had begun at Tamoanchán had been transferred to Teotihuacán. There the gods met to decide who was to sacrifice himself so as to become the new, the fifth, sun and bring light again to the world:

> *Even though it was night,*
> *even though it was not day,*
> *even though there was no light,*
> *they gathered,*
> *the gods convened*
> *there in Teotihuacán.*[2]

The most humble of them all, the 'Purulent One', cast himself into the flames and became the sun. But the heavenly bodies did not move, so *all* the gods sacrificed themselves for mankind. Finally, government was established there; the lords of Teotihuacán were 'wise men, knowers of occult things, possessors of the traditions'. When they died, pyramids were built above them. The largest of the pyramids, those of the Sun and Moon, were said by tradition to have been built by the giants which existed in those days (thus the legend naïvely says, 'It is not unbelievable that they were made by hand').

The Valley of Teotihuacán is actually a side pocket of the Valley of Mexico, comprising about 100 square miles of bottom land lying to the north east of the Valley proper and surrounded by hills. Of this, about one half is suitable for farming. Springs produce copious water which could have been used by the Teotihuacanos for irrigation, but there is no proof that they ever did.

A photogrammetric mapping project carried out by René Millon of the University of Rochester gives an idea of the gigantic size of this metropolis. It covers over 9 square miles and was fully urbanised. Teotihuacán was laid out shortly after the time of Christ on a grid plan which is consistently oriented to 15 degrees 30 minutes east of true north, arguing that the planners must have been sophisticated surveyors as well. Its major axis is the Avenue of the Dead, which used to be thought to end at the so-called 'Ciudadela' in the south, a distance of two miles from its northern terminus at the Pyramid of the Moon. It is now known that the avenue is *twice* this length; and that it is bisected at the Ciudadela

Plate 27

by an east–west avenue of equal length, so that the city was laid out in quarters.

Teotihuacán was first settled during the Late Formative (Teo⁄tihuacán I phase), when the plan must have been developed, but the city as it now stands is entirely of the Proto⁄Classic (Teotihuacán II) and Early Classic (Teotihuacán III) periods. By A D 500 it had reached the height of its population, probably around 150,000 to 200,000 persons, making Teotihuacán in its hey⁄day one of the largest contemporary cities in the world.

The Pyramids of the Sun and of the Moon are explicitly named in old legends, and there can be no reason to doubt that they were dedicated to

Plate 28

those divinities. The former lies to the east of the Avenue of the Dead and not far from it. Its sides 700 feet long and a little over 200 feet high, it towers above the surrounding mounds and other ruins. Within it, at the base, is an earlier platform, but the great four⁄sided pyramid itself was raised in stages during late Teotihuacán I, and probably Teotihuacán II times. The interior fill is formed entirely of sun⁄dried bricks made from mud, more than one million cubic yards of it. The exterior was once entirely faced with stone, and it rose in five great bodies. A stone stairway, in part bifurcated, led to a wood⁄and⁄thatch temple on its lofty summit. The Pyramid of the Moon was broadly similar, although smaller. Both structures attest the immense power of the Teotihuacán hierarchy to call up corvée labour from the villages of the territory over which it ruled. It has been pointed out that in the absence of advanced technology, a powerful state must rely on the work of such 'human ants'.

Classic Teotihuacán architecture is based on a few simple principles. Interiors of adobe bricks or small stones are faced with broken⁄up volcanic stones set in clay and covered with a smooth coat of lime plaster. The typical architectural motif is that known as *talud⁄tablero*: a rectangular panel with inset is placed over a sloping wall. Even the tiers of the Pyramid of the Sun are believed to have had this form.

Apart from the great pyramids, most of the buildings excavated at Teotihuacán are palaces, the residences of the lords of the city, such as those uncovered at the zones called by the modern names Xolálpan, Tetitla, Tepantitla, Zacuala, and Atetelco. Typical of the palace layout might be Xolálpan, a rectangular complex of about 45 rooms and seven forecourts; these border four platforms, which are arranged around a

*Fig. 23. Representation of a temple
on a Teotihuacán pottery vessel of
the Early Classic Period*

central court. The court was depressed below the general ground level and was open to the sky, with a small altar in the centre. While windows were lacking, several of the rooms have smaller sunken courts very much like *atria*, into which light and air were admitted through the roof, supported by surrounding columns. The rain water in the sunken basins could be drained off when desired. All palaces known were one-storied affairs, with flat roofs built from beams and small sticks and twigs, overlain by earth and rubble. Doorways were rectangular and covered by a cloth.

Something of the sophistication and artistry of the Teotihuacanos can be seen in the magnificent frescoes, usually of gods, which adorn the walls of the palaces. In the porticoes of one of the buildings in the White Patio at Atetelco are depicted processions of jaguars and coyotes, painted in various shades of red, and perhaps symbolising knightly orders. The most famous of the palace murals are those at Tepantitla, where a large fresco in blue, red, yellow, and brown covering an entire wall represents the Paradise of the Rain God, or to use the Náhuatl term, *Tlalocan*. The tableau is dominated by the deity himself. Drops of water flow from his hands, while in a fanciful landscape little human figures frolic, sing, and play games. Butterflies and flowering trees add to the general gaiety of the scene, an evocation of the heaven to which were translated those who had drowned or otherwise died by water.

None of these palaces are of sufficient size to have been the abode of the supreme ruler of the city. The interesting suggestion has been made by Pedro Armillas that the so-called Ciudadela, a roughly square enclosure with sides over 700 yards long at the centre of the city, was the royal palace itself, since it conforms to the descriptions of such which we have

Fig. 24
Plate 32

Plate 27

Fig. 24. Reconstruction of the White Patio, in a palace at Atet-elco, Teotihuacán. Early Classic Period. Width of floor between the stairways of the two flanking buildings, 28 ft

from the time of the Conquest in the Valley of Mexico. Within the Ciudadela, on the eastern side of the inner plaza, is the Temple of Quetzalcóatl, a six-tiered step-pyramid with typical *talud-tablero* façades, constructed at the beginning of the Early Classic period and partly covered by a later pyramid. Around the stone cornices sculptured Feathered Serpents alternate with heads of the Fire Serpent, bearer of the sun on its daily journey across the heavens; effigy sea shells have been added as water symbols. If this complex really was the royal palace, then the official cult may have been that of Quetzalcóatl himself.

If palaces alone had been built in ancient Teotihuacán, this would have been a peculiar sort of city. Some idea of the way more ordinary people lived is given by the extraordinary ruin discovered by Linné at the

Fig. 25

location in the eastern part of the site called Tlamimilolpa. This was a crowded cluster of rooms and alleys; although the ultimate extent of this complex was never determined due to lack of time, no fewer than 176 rooms, 21 forecourts (*atria*), and five courtyards were uncovered. Not all rooms were interconnected, and apparently groups of these formed private apartments. As yet we do not know to what degree Tlamimil⁄ olpa was typical of the city as a whole, but there must have been an immense multitude of traders, artisans, and other non⁄food producers living in quarters of this sort. Mexico was to see nothing like this until the Aztecs built their capital Tenochtitlán.

Many of the gods of the complete Mexican pantheon are already clearly recognisable at Teotihuacán. Here were worshipped above all the

93

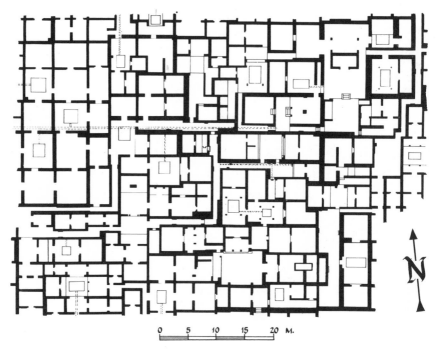

Fig. 25. *Plan of building complex found at Tlamimilolpa, Teotihuacán. After Linné*

Fig. 26

Rain God and the Feathered Serpent, as well as the Sun God, the Moon Goddess, and Xipe Totec, the last-named being the symbol of the annual renewal of the vegetation. A colossal statue of stone represents the

Plate 29 Water Goddess (in Náhuatl, Chalchihuitlícue, 'the lady of the jade skirts'). Note that almost all those venerated in this great urban capital were intimately concerned with the well-being of the maize, with their staff of life.

Tradition holds that this was a sacred burial ground. Really important tombs have seemingly been discovered only by professional treasure hunters, but underneath the floors of the palaces and apartment buildings have been encountered a number of slab-lined graves. The Teotihuacanos like the later Aztecs favoured cremation of the dead, the body first being wrapped in a bundle. Around the remains were placed fine offerings of all sorts, particularly lovely and graceful vases, obsidian artifacts, and perishable things like textiles. Beliefs about the hereafter are recorded in a Náhuatl song:

> *And they called it Teotihuacán*
> *because it was the place*
> *where the lords were buried.*
> *Thus they said:*
> *'When we die,*
> *truly we die not,*
> *because we will live, we will rise,*
> *we will continue living, we will awaken.*
> *This will make us happy.'*
> *Thus the dead one was directed,*
> *when he died:*
> *'Awaken, already the sky is rosy,*
> *already sing the flame-coloured guans,*
> *the fire-coloured swallows,*
> *already the butterflies fly.'*
> *Thus the old ones said*
> *that who has died has become a god,*
> *they said: 'He has been made a god there,'*
> *meaning, 'He has died.'*[3]

The Teotihuacán art style as revealed in their frescoes, sculpture, pottery, and other productions is tremendously elegant and refined, as well as highly stylised and ordered. Sculpture is best represented in the austere stone masks, fashioned from greenstone, basalt, jade, andesite and other materials, each of which once had inlaid eyes of mussel-shells or obsidian, as well as in a few very large-scale pieces such as the Water Goddess.

Plate 31

The hallmark of the Teotihuacán culture is the cylindrical pottery vase with three, slab-shaped feet. These vases usually have fitted lids on top with handles in the form of a bird. Other characteristic forms in clay include vessels shaped like flower vases. Decoration on these luxury items, found in graves and far away as trade pieces, commonly is plano-relief, with the cut-away areas painted with vermilion, although the finest

Fig. 27

have been stuccoed and painted with sacred scenes in the same manner as the wall frescoes. A fine ware known as Thin Orange was also of local manufacture, appearing as bowls with annular bases, boxes with lids, or effigies of little dogs.

Other objects of clay include large polychromed incense burners, built up of mould-made details, mould-made figurines of men and gods, and little two-holed *candeleros*, which might have been used to contain blood offered to the gods in an act of self-sacrifice. Clay pellets were *Fig. 28* carefully shaped for employment as blow-gun missiles, and we know from a scene on a vase that this weapon was used in hunting birds.

Obsidian chipping reached new heights of elaboration, with the *Fig. 29* production of spear and dart points as well as little human effigies of that material. As usual, vast quantities of razor-like blades of obsidian are present. The Teotihuacán state controlled the great obsidian deposits near Pachuca, Hidalgo; and the 350 obsidian workshops known to

Fig. 26. Tlaloc, God of Rain, from a fresco on a palace wall at Zacuala, Teotihuacán

96

Fig. 27. Ceramics from Early Classic burials at Teotihuacán. a–b, cylindrical tripods decorated in carved relief technique; c, florero; d, 'cream pitcher'; e, jar with face of Tlaloc; f–g, candeleros; h–i, Thin Orange ware. 1/4

have existed in the city were probably the mercantile basis on which this urban centre rested.

Bone needles and bodkins testify to the manufacture of clothing and basketry, and we have the charred remains of cotton and agave fibre cloth with weft pattern, coiled baskets, and twilled sleeping mats or *petates*.

97

Fig. 28. Fragment of cylindrical tripod vessel with relief design of blowgunner hunting quetzal birds in a cacao tree. From Teotihuacán, Early Classic Period. Height 4⅜ in.

Paintings show that men wore a loin-cloth and/or kilt with sandals, and women the pull-over *huipil* and underskirt.

Although none have survived, books must have been in both ritual and administrative use, for these people had writing. From the few isolated glyphs which have been identified on the pottery and in the frescoes, it is known that they had bar-and-dot numeration and used the 260-day count (Almanac Year).

The city that we have described held sway over most of the central highlands of Mexico during the Early Classic. Teotihuacán influence is

The Urban Civilisation of Teotihuacán

strong even in more remote regions, such as the Gulf Coast, Oaxaca, *cf. Fig. 22*
and the Maya area. Elegant vases of pure Teotihuacán manufacture are
found in the burials of nobles all over Mexico at this time, and the art of
the Teotihuacanos dominated the germinating styles of the other high
civilisations of Mesoamerica. Six hundred and fifty miles to the south-
east, in the highlands of Guatemala on the outskirts of the modern
capital of that republic, a little 'city' has been found that is in all respects a
miniature copy of Teotihuacán. The tombs of the chiefs of this centre,
Kaminaljuyú, are full of luxuries from Teotihuacán itself, and it is
considered probable that these leaders were invaders from that great
Mexican city. A similar situation has been found at that colossus of
Maya centres, Tikal, situated in the lowland jungle of northern
Guatemala, where an Early Classic stela shows a jade-bedecked ruler
flanked by what seem to be two mercenaries from Teotihuacán.

The question is, and it must be admitted that no definite answer can
be given, who were the people of Teotihuacán? Who built this city, and
whence did they come? The early Spanish historian Torquemada tells us
that the Totonac claimed the honour, and in this light it is true that the
earliest Classic Teotihuacán buildings show a certain decorative
influence from Veracruz, the Totonac homeland. Some scholars claim
an Otomí occupation of the city, others hold for the Popoloca. In view of
the strong continuities between Teotihuacán on the one hand and the
Toltecs and Aztecs on the other, in both sacred and secular features, the
Nahua affinities of this civilisation would appear to be the most
probable. On this question we are little wiser than were the native

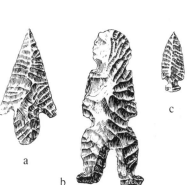

Fig. 29. Chipped obsidian artifacts from Early Classic Period at Teotihuacán. a, c and d, spear and dart points. 3/8; b, human effigy, 3/4

99

peoples, who thought that Teotihuacán had been built by giants or gods.

The city met its end through deliberate destruction and burning by the hand of unknown invaders. These might have been Otomí-speaking nomads from the outer marches of civilisation, from the great semi-deserts of the north and north-west, whence came most of the later incursions into the heart of Mexico. By about A D 600, all Teotihuacán influence over the rest of Mesoamerica suddenly ceases. No more do the nobility of other states stock their tombs with the refined products of the great city. The luxurious palaces of Teotihuacán were now in ruins, and squatters were living within jerry-built walls thrown across the floors, sometimes placing their dead beneath the old rooms like the former inhabitants. This barbaric occupation persisted for about 300 years after the fall of the city, during which a red-on-buff pottery called Coyotlatelco was manufactured, no rival of the beautiful wares of the Teotihuacanos, but in part fashioned on their model. Refugees from the city are thought to have removed to the relatively small centre of Atzcapotzalco, west of the great lake, futilely carrying on an epigonal version of their old culture.

A mighty crisis overtook all the Classic civilisations of Mesoamerica towards the end of the ninth century A D, the most drastic convulsion being reserved for the Classic Maya, who were forced to abandon most of their centres. In the Valley of Teotihuacán, this event took place some three centuries earlier, forcing the collapse of civilised life in most of central Mexico before the Late Classic period had really begun elsewhere. Vaillant proposed that the destruction of the surrounding forests necessary for the burning of the lime that went into the building of Teotihuacán resulted in a precocious erosion and desiccation of the region. A related factor might have been the increasing aridity of the climate all over Mexico during the Classic, which apparently was severest in the Valley of Mexico. The whole edifice of the Teotihuacán state may have perished through the ensuing agricultural débâcle, opening civilised Mexico to nomadic tribes from the northern frontier.

THE GREAT PYRAMID OF CHOLULA

As the present-day traveller leaves the Valley of Mexico and journeys south-east across the mountains rimming the basin, he eventually drops down on to the plains of Puebla, the volcanic peaks of Iztaccíhuatl and Popocatépetl rising on his right hand. Once on the plain itself, he sees before him shining in the sun the yellow-and-green tiled domes of a Colonial period church which seems to rest on a very large hill. It comes as a shock to realise that this is not a hill at all, but a man-made pyramid, that of Cholula, the largest ancient structure in the New World, and sacred to the god Quetzalcóatl.

Plate 30

The Great Pyramid, which was already in ruins when the Spaniards first arrived, is actually the result of four successive superpositions, all carried out during the Classic period, using mud bricks as fill. The earliest pyramids exhibit strong Teotihuacán influence, with the characteristic *talud-tablero* motif of that site, and one is painted with insect-like designs in pure Classic Teotihuacán style. Following the withering of Teotihuacán hegemony over central Mexico, the builders of Cholula worked in an increasingly independent style, and the pyramid in its final form shows few traits from further north. In its last state, the Great Pyramid is incredibly massive: it covers an area of 25 acres and is 180 feet high. To the Post-Classic Mexicans, who maintained a vigorous culture in the region, it was one of the wonders of their country and memories yet persisted of its traditional dedication to the Feathered Serpent.

CERRO DE LA MESAS

Down on the Gulf Coast plain, new civilisations appeared in the Early Classic which in some respects reflect continuity from the old Olmec tradition of the lowlands, as well as intrusive elements ultimately derived from Teotihuacán. The site of Cerro de las Mesas lies in the middle of the former Olmec territory, in south-central Veracruz, approximately 15 miles from the Bay of Alvarado, on a broad band of high land above the swamps of the Río Blanco. The site is the centre of an area dotted with earthen mounds. Cerro de las Mesas was occupied from Middle Formative through Late Post-Classic times, but attained its apogee during the Early Classic.

A number of stelae encountered there by Stirling show features recalling both the Olmec and Izapan styles. One side of each monument is generally carved in low relief so as to depict a hieratically posed personage in rich attire, in profile with one leg stiffly outstretched before

Plate 33

the other. The Olmec were-jaguar appears in mask-like headdresses and on half-masks which are occasionally worn over the lower face. Two of the monuments record Long Count dates, one being 9.1.12.14.10 (AD 468) and the other 9.4.18.16.8 (AD 533), well within the AD 300–600 span of the Early Classic. Other sculptures include a monstrous figure of a duck-billed human closely resembling the Tuxtla Statuette, which itself was found not very far from Cerro de las Mesas.

cf. Fig. 19

Excavations in the site brought to light a fantastically rich cache of carved jade. Altogether there were 782 pieces, buried together at some time in the Early Classic. While some are very much of the period, especially those in the local styles of the Maya highlands and of Oaxaca, a good number are purely Olmec, obviously heirlooms handed down from the ancient civilisation that had once controlled this region. Was this cache left by some trafficker in fine jewellery? Does it represent the hoard of some local prince? Or, most plausible of all, is this an offering to the unknown gods of Cerro de las Mesas?

THE CLASSIC VERACRUZ CIVILISATION

A large number of fine stone objects found on the Gulf Coast plain are carved in a very distinct style that has become known as 'Classic Veracruz'. The majority of them are from the northern and central parts of that state, a zone in which are located several great élite centres which shared in the same art tradition. This style can be mistaken for no other in Mexico; on the contrary, its closest affinities seem to lie, for no apparent reason, across the Pacific with the Bronze and Iron Age cultures of China. It is a style in which all subject matter is secondary and bound to a complex ornamental motif, one of linked or intertwined scrolls with raised edges, perhaps the offspring of the cloud scrolls of the Izapan style.

Plate 34

The Classic Veracruz style commonly appears on a complex of enigmatic stone objects, the so-called 'yokes', *palmas*, and *hachas* ('axes' or thin stone heads). Modern research has shown that all three are associated with the ritual ball game, as bas-reliefs and figurines depict them being worn in that connection. The 'yokes', which are U-shaped and intricately carved to represent stylised toads covered with convoluted scrolls and human faces, were stone replicas of the heavy protective belts worn by the players. At the front of this ceremonial belt was fitted the

Plate 40

Fig. 30. Stela in Classic
Veracruz style, Late
Classic Period, from
Aparicio, Veracruz.
Represented is a seated
ball player, complete with
palma; his head has been
severed, and seven
intertwined snakes sprout
from the neck

palma, an elongated sculpture adapted for that purpose; palmas are often
effigies of birds like turkeys, or are carved with realistic scenes. The thin
stone heads probably were markers placed in the court to score the game.
In its formative phase, the style can best be seen in slate backs for circular

Plate 38

Plate 37

Plate 34

mirrors of pyrite mosaic – these are certainly Early Classic in date, as are most of the 'yokes'.

The tribal name 'Totonac' has often been inappropriately applied to these carvings; while it is true that the Totonac now occupy most of the zone in which such remains are found, it may or may not have been they who made them. Archaeologists prefer caution in these matters. Nevertheless, Classic Veracruz influence is very perceptibly present in the beginnings of Classic Teotihuacán, and some are inclined to accept Torquemada's statement that these people built that city. On the other hand, reciprocal influence from the highlands is also present, here on the Gulf Coast.

In accord with the importance of ball court equipment in their art, there are no less than seven ball courts at the most important Classic Veracruz site, El Tajín, an élite centre about five miles south-west of Papantla, in the rich oil-producing zone of northern Veracruz. The surrounding land is highly fertile for maize, cacao, and vanilla, all of which are still grown. The site derives its name from the belief of the modern Totonac that twelve old men called *Tajín* live in the ruins and are lords of the thunderstorm (and therefore the equivalent of the Rain God).

El Tajín is very extensive, its nucleus covering about 146 acres, but subsidiary ruins are scattered over several thousand acres. The site is set among low hills and part of it has been built up with artificial platforms to compensate for the slope. The centre may have been first occupied in the Early Classic, but the peak activity was towards the close of the Late Classic (A D 600–900), and perhaps even slightly after. Much of El Tajín has never been excavated, but the structures already cleared are striking.

Plate 35

The Pyramid of the Niches is a relatively small (only about 60 feet high), four-sided structure of wonderful symmetry, faced with carved stone blocks, rising in six tiers to an upper sanctuary. A single stairway climbs to the top, flanked by balustrades embellished with a step-and-fret motif. Around the sides are a number of small square niches, 365 in all, the number of days in the solar year. Inside the pyramid has been discovered a more ancient one, almost a duplicate of the outer.

Other stone buildings at El Tajín are very similar in construction, the step-and-fret design being particularly common. Palace-like buildings with colonnaded doorways were roofed with massive concrete slabs (utilising marine shell and sand cement mixed with pumice and wood fragments) poured over wooden scaffolds, rather an advanced con, struction technique for the day. The Building of the Columns is the largest complex at the site; the drums of the columns are carved in reliefs showing winged dancers, Eagle Knights, human sacrifices, and bar, and, dot numerals with day glyphs, testifying to the literacy of this civilisation.

Above all, the inhabitants of El Tajín were obsessed with the ball game, human sacrifice, and death, three concepts closely interwoven in the Mexican mind. The courts, which are up to 197 feet long, are formed by two facing walls, with stone surfaces either vertical or battered. Magnificent bas, reliefs in some of them are witnesses of the drama of the game, for a few scenes show ceremonies involving the players in the court itself, all wearing the appropriate paraphernalia. In one relief, over which Plate 39 the Death God presides, the losing captain is apparently being sacrificed by the victors, who brandish a flint knife over his heart: the game played in the courts of El Tajín was not lightly won or lost. The Death God is ubiquitous at the site, his fleshless skull and skeleton found in both free Plate 36 sculpture and in relief, his bony spine a common architectural motif.

El Tajín probably managed to survive the unsettled transition between the end of the Classic and the beginning of the more militaristic Post, Classic. Its destruction was by fire, and tradition has it that the zone was conquered by the 'Chichimecs', nomadic barbarians from the highlands, at the outset of the thirteenth century A D.

REMOJADAS POTTERS

An exuberant style in pottery sprang up during the Classic period in a zone of central Veracruz fronting the Gulf of Mexico near the modern port capital of the state. Named Remojadas from the site at which they are most abundant, tens of thousands of hollow clay figurines were fashioned in a naturalistic style from which much ethnographic data can Plate 41 be drawn. The roots of the art reach back to the Late Formative, but most production was during the Late Classic, when Remojadas figurines have some kinship with those of the Classic Maya to the east. Features such as faces were generally cast from clay moulds, and a black asphalt paint was used to heighten details or to indicate face paint. The

Plate 42

Plate 43

subjects are standing or seated humans, both male and female: curiously infantile boys and girls with laughing faces and filed teeth; ball players; lovers or friends in swings; and warriors. The gods are also portrayed: the native Gulf Coast deity, Xipe Totec, as represented by a priest wearing the skin of a flayed captive; the Death God; and probably Quetzalcóatl in his guise as god of wind. The vessels associated with these figurines are generally simple, deep bowls, occasionally with a pleasant polychrome ornamentation.

CLASSIC MONTE ALBAN

The civilisation of Monte Albán in the Valley of Oaxaca during Classic times was almost certainly the product of Zapotecan-speaking peoples. The change-over from the Late Formative appears to have been peaceful, with some new elements in the Proto-Classic Monte Albán II coming up from the Maya area as a kind of burial cult: potstands, painted stucco decoration of pottery, and so forth. But Maya influence stops with the commencement of the Classic proper, and a new series of cultural elements holds sway, particularly strong influence being exerted by Teotihuacán. There is no reason to think, however, of any major shift in population or of outside invasion. Furthermore, Oaxaca was sufficiently isolated to avoid the troubles visited upon Teotihuacán during the Classic period. The shift from Early (Monte Albán III-A) to Late Classic (Monte Albán III-B) is thus hardly perceptible here. Left to themselves to populate their own territory, the Zapotecs built site after site; while in Monte Albán II only 18 or 19 sites are known, by the close of the Classic there were no less than 200 in the Valley of Oaxaca.

Plate 45

The Classic site as it now stands was developed around a very large and long plaza. Bigger constructions were raised on rock nuclei that remained after the hill was levelled off. Among the buildings of this epoch are stone-faced platforms, fronted by stairways with flanking balustrades. Something like the *talud-tablero* architecture of Teotihuacán is evident, but the panel is modified from its original form. These and other buildings were once stuccoed and beautifully painted. Also present is a magnificent masonry ball court with a ground plan like a capital 'I'; above the sloping playing surfaces are what look like stone grandstands for the spectators.

Fig. 31. Part of painting on walls of Tomb 104 at Monte Albán, Oaxaca. Early in Monte Albán III-B culture, c. A D 600. The Young Maize God appears on the right. Height of wall 5 ft 3 in.

Subterranean tombs have been discovered all over the site, some of which were of great magnificence, testimony of the wealth of the lords of Monte Albán. The best are quite elaborate chambers, often with a corbelled vault, and have an ante-chamber. Fine frescoes were painted on the plastered walls. Tomb 104, in the northern part of the site, is certainly the most spectacular known thus far. Over the façade of the tomb, which is a miniature reproduction of a temple, is a niche containing a pottery urn representing a person wearing the headdress of the Rain God. The door was a single great slab covered with hieroglyphs; within the funerary chamber the skeleton was stretched out on the floor, surrounded by rich offerings including more clay urns. Hurriedly painted while the deceased awaited burial are lovely frescoes

Fig. 31

which grace the walls, depicting a procession of gods advancing towards the rear of the tomb, interspaced with glyphs. The style of these and other Classic Monte Albán frescoes, down to the smallest details such as treatment of the feather ornamentation, is obviously derivative from Teotihuacán.

Some, at least, of the gods of Monte Albán are shared with other Mexican peoples and can thus be identified. Their divinity finds abundant expression in the numberless pottery urns placed with the dead, often in groups. In these, the use of the mould is eschewed, much of the ornamentation being built up by sharply carved clay strips. Each god is generally shown as seated cross-legged, richly dressed with an elaborate headdress containing the symbol by which he is known. We have in an old dictionary the Zapotec names of some of these deities. The most important member of the pantheon was the Rain God, *Cocijo*; the Maize God, *Pitao Cozobi*, often adorned with actual casts of maize ears; the Feathered Serpent; a Bat God, best represented by a sinister-looking jade-and-shell mosaic pendant of Monte Albán II date; the Old Fire God; and, possibly, the Water Goddess.

A large group of gods and goddesses are only identified by their calendrical names, and their exact role remains unknown. The writing and calendric system of Classic Monte Albán was fully developed from the Formative base. Although there are no surviving codices, glyphs appear everywhere, both in sculptured relief, on the funerary urns, and painted on walls, at the principal site itself and at other Monte Albán centres. The numeration continues to be in the bar-and-dot system; dates were written with the day signs of the Almanac Year, but also in terms of the Solar Year. As might be expected, there is some resemblance to Teotihuacán in these glyphs. Many of the inscriptions are very long; but, beyond the dates, very little else can yet be deciphered.

We have said that Teotihuacán was the only real city in Classic Mexico, and that Monte Albán is of the more typical kind of settlement, that is, an élite centre. It is true that there is no possibility there of a dense congregation of persons living cheek-by-jowl. Nevertheless, the slopes of the tall hill on which the site is located have been converted into terraces, and aerial photographs show the possibility of residential houses clustering on these. Were these priests, merchants, artisans, politicians? Whoever they were, by the end of Monte Albán III-B about A D 900 all

Plate 44

inhabitants had left Monte Albán, and this and other centres of civilisation in the Valley of Oaxaca fell gradually into ruin. Later peoples, like the Mixtecs, used the old Zapotec site as a kind of consecrated ground for their tombs, some of them as we shall see, quite wonderful, perhaps in an attempt to establish their continuity with the native dynasties which had ruled here for over a thousand years.

WESTERN MEXICO

It would be stretching a term unduly to call the various cultures of western Mexico which we *think* belong to the AD 100–900 period 'civilised', or in any respect the equal of the other great Classic cultures which we have examined. Apparently beyond the confines of literate civilisation, a series of peasant groups in this region produced some pleasant *objets d'art* which are often decorative but hardly in the class of Teotihuacán, El Tajín, or Monte Albán.

The rather dry basin of the upper Balsas River, in the state of Guerrero, is a rich source for portable objects in Olmec style. After the Formative, and perhaps developing out of an Olmec substream, appears the style called Mezcala, and known only from carved pieces of andesite and serpentine recovered by illegal pot-hunting. These objects are highly abstract, usually representations of human figures recalling in pose and technique the simpler small productions of Teotihuacán. As well as these, miniature façades of colonnaded temples are also known, and a few effigies of natural objects like conch shells. The exact dating and cultural context of Mezcala art will be known only when scientific excavation is undertaken in the area, but a Late Formative or Early Classic placement now seems reasonable.

Plate 46

Plate 47

Nayarit, Jalisco, and Colima are three contiguous states on the Pacific coast between Guerrero and the Gulf of California. Here a number of local centres produced a surprising range of genre art in clay, some of it showing a lively sense of humour, making this the western counterpart of the Remojadas culture of Veracruz, but different from it in the absence of the mould. Some of these handmade clay figures and vessels are thought to be Classic in date on the ground of a certain tenuous resemblance of some forms to Teotihuacán pottery, but we really are almost entirely ignorant of the archaeology of the region. It is said that most of the

Plate 48

Plate 49

Plate 50

Plate 51

thousands of pieces in collections were recovered by local treasure-seekers in deep, multichambered tombs reached by shafts.

Nayarit, particularly the neighbourhood around Ixtlán del Río, specialised in lively figures and groups painted in black, white, and yellow on a reddish ground. The subjects are men and women in naturalistic poses, some playing flutes or beating turtle-shell drums; warriors brandishing clubs; temples with thatched roofs; houses and even villages; and ball courts with the game actually going on. Although artistically of little note, the anecdotal nature of the scenes renders them of great ethnological interest, for much of the everyday life of ancient Mexico is here revealed in startling detail.

A more sophisticated and polished art in clay was produced by Jalisco and Colima. Especially famous are the little pot-bellied dogs of Colima belonging to the hairless breed that the Mexicans specially fattened for consumption by forced feeding like Strasbourg geese; these are depicted sleeping, playing, growling, and in many other moods. Other vessels represent various kinds of birds, hunchbacks, and all the variety of human life that interested these potters. Particularly attractive are the red ware pots enclosed by water-lily petals, borne by legs in the form of birds or atlantean humans.

THE CLASSIC DOWNFALL

The single most important fact which archaeologists have learned about the Classic period in Mexico is the supremacy of Teotihuacán, its impress being clearly recorded throughout this incredibly varied country. As the urbanised centre of Mexico, with high population and tremendous production, its power was imposed through political and cultural means not only in its native highland habitat, but also along the tropical coasts, reaching even into the Maya area. That this was an empire entirely comparable with the Aztec cannot be doubted. In fact, it may have been even bigger than that of Moctezuma II. All other states were partly or entirely dependent upon it for whatever achievements they attained at this time, and any solution of the problem of why the Classic developed at all must be approached through the more central problem that Teotihuacán, without local antecedents, presents to puzzled archaeologists.

When Teotihuacán fell, the unifying force in Mexico was gone, and with it widespread interregional trade. The Late Classic saw an increasing fractionalisation, each culture moving along its own lines, effectively cut off from the others. These other Classic civilisations fell 300 years later than did Teotihuacán, probably as a result of a combination of agricultural collapse through drought and the pressure of outer barbarians, who we know were then knocking at the gates of civilised Mexico. It is as if the pattern of Mexican life, established with the first civilisations of the Formative, had become exhausted. Perhaps the weary farmers of Mexico were no longer willing to build pyramids and palaces for leaders who failed to provide the rains that would guarantee them full harvests.

In short, the country was ripe for revolution as well as conquest from outside, and the two forces probably together produced the radically different way of life that we see in the Post-Classic period.

CHAPTER VII

The Post-Classic Period: Early Militarists

A TIME OF TROUBLES

Following in the wake of the widespread disturbances which brought to a close the civilisations of the Classic around the end of the ninth century A D was an entirely new mode of organised life. The salient characteristic of this age, the Post-Classic, was a new militarism, in fact, a glorification of war in all its aspects. The intellectual hierarchy of the older cultures had now either disappeared or was relegated to inferior status. In its place was an upstart class of tough professional warriors, grouped into military orders which took their names from the animals from which they may have claimed a kind of totemic descent: coyote, jaguar, and eagle. Wars were the rule of the day, those unfortunate enough to be captured destined for sacrifice to gods who were now hungry for the taste of human blood. As a result, for the first time in Mexico there was a need for the construction of strongpoints and the fortification of towns.

Throughout Mexico, this was a time which saw a great deal of confusion and movement of peoples, amalgamating to form small, aggressive, conquest states, and splitting up with as much speed as they had risen. Even tribes of distinctly different speech sometimes came together to form a single state – as we know from their annals, for we have here entered the realm of history.

Some of these parvenus created troubles over a very wide area within Mexico; prime among them were a mixed Nahua-Mixtec people known as the Olmeca (not to be confused with the 'Olmecs' of the Gulf Coast), who suddenly conquered Cholula in Puebla around A D 800, setting up a powerful despotism there and reaching north to the Valley of Mexico in an attempt to subjugate all of the central highlands. It is just at this time that the first fortifications about which we know were thrown up around the élite centre of Xochicalco, strategically placed atop one of a string of hills in southern Morelos, probably guarding against the northern thrust of the Olmeca. Xochicalco appears to lie at the break

Plate 52

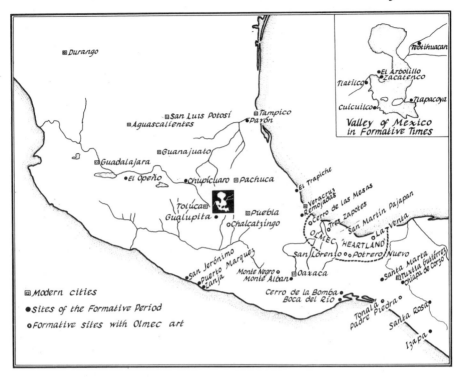

Fig. 32. Distribution of Toltec sites and other important centres of the Post-Classic Period. The inset map is the Valley of Mexico

between the Classic and Post-Classic periods; while on the one hand its pyramid with bas-reliefs of the Feathered Serpent and seated nobles reflects the influence of the Classic Maya far to the south, its defensive ditches and concentric ramparts testify to its survival into a more sanguinary period.

Naturally, such new conditions are mirrored in Post-Classic art styles, which are thoroughly saturated with the martial psychology of the age. In general they are harder, far more abstract, and less exuberant than those of the Classic period. It is the kind of strong, static art produced by craftsmen guided by Spartan, not Athenian, ideals.

The introduction of metallurgy into Mexico took place at about the beginning of the Post-Classic period, but had only a slight effect upon the development of native civilisation, in contrast to its history in the Old World. The first metal objects, almost entirely of copper, appear on the west coast of the Republic, making it a certainty that the art was spread north from the Andean Area by sea traders plying along the Pacific coast, for objects from either region are extraordinarily similar in both technique

Plate 60

and form. Mexican metalwork largely consists of ornaments, particularly small bells cast by the 'lost wax' method, while implements such as celts or axes are relatively rare and so had little significance in the native tool kit, which remained on an essentially Neolithic level. In the realm of jewellery, however, the craftsmanship of the Mexican goldsmith reached heights of great artistry, as we shall see.

THE NORTHERN BARBARIANS

It was not only internal pressure brought by new conquest states that disturbed Mexico. Probably more far-reaching in their long-range effects

Fig. 32

were the great migrations into Mexico by barbaric tribes inhabiting the wastelands beyond the northern limits of Mesoamerican farming. The Aztecs called all of the northerners beyond the pale of civilised life 'Chichimeca', a name meaning something like 'lineage of the dog', not a term of opprobrium since several ruling dynasties in the valley of Mexico were proud to claim Chichimec ancestry. These barbarians were nomadic hunters who carried their bows and arrows everywhere with them and knew not how to cultivate the land. In the account recorded by Father Sahagún, wildest of all were the 'Teochichimeca', the 'real' Chichimeca, who lived in caves and clothed themselves in animal skins and yucca-fibre sandals, subsisting on wild fruits, roots, and seeds and on the meat of humble animals like the rabbit. Between them and the civilised peoples were the 'Tamime', Chichimeca who had picked up a smattering of the customs and speech of their more advanced neighbours to the south; they wore the cast-off rags of civilisation and did a little farming to supplement their wild diet.

Who in fact were the Chichimeca? The inner plateau of northern

Fig. 1

Mexico is a vast rocky desert bordered on the west and east by the two Sierra Madre ranges. Here lived until recent times primitive tribes like the Uto-Aztecan speaking Zacateca and Tepehuan, the Guachichil of unknown affiliation, and the Pame. These peoples were, then, exactly what the Aztecs meant by 'Teochichimeca'. The heirs of the old 'Desert Culture', forbidden tillage of the soil because of low rainfall, they were mainly collectors of mesquite seeds and hunters of rabbits, which were caught in communal drives. Being perforce semi-nomadic, they travelled in small bands under the leadership of a headman and lived, like the Chichimeca, in either caves or else dome-shaped brush shelters. Lacking from their simple religions were temples, idols, and priests. Most were unfamiliar with pottery or the loom. Easily recognisable here is a mode of existence shared with desert-living Indians as far north as Oregon and one recalling the Archaic background of Mexican civilisation.

Dependent upon fluctuations in rainfall, the northern border of Mesoamerica actually wavered back and forth over the centuries, as farmers moved north or were forced back by drought. One long, narrow band of cultivators extended along the moist eastern slopes of the Sierra Madre Occidental almost to the American South-west; another lay to the west of these mountains, on the coast of western Mexico to the Gulf of California. The peoples of these two strips were not particularly advanced. On the contrary, their position as farmers was rather precarious and they of necessity possessed some of the characteristics of the nomads, just as the frontiersmen of the American West adopted Indian customs as their own. In other words, they were 'semi-Chichimeca' like those Tamime described by Sahagún.

In general, the northerners, like all Desert Culture tribes, were quite peaceful. This was especially so when desert conditions were relatively good; then, increased precipitation brought in farmers from the south and the frontiers marched forward. When, however, the reverse was true, the wild nomads, driven to desperation by drought and starvation, pushed south into regions that were formerly occupied by tillers of the soil, raiding the outposts of civilisation. Then, even the part farmers of the north were pushed back. This would account for the great Chichimec invasions which took place in the Post-Classic period.

TULA AND THE TOLTECS

There have been only three unifying forces in the pre-Spanish history of Mexico: the first of these was Classic Teotihuacán, the second the

Toltecs, and the last was the Aztec state. In their own annals, written down in Spanish letters after the Conquest, the Mexican nobility and intelligentsia looked back in wonder to an almost semi-mythical time when the Toltecs ruled, a people whose very name means 'the artificers'. Of them it was said that 'nothing was too difficult for them, no place with which they dealt was too distant'. From their capital, Tula, they had dominated much of northern and central Mexico in ancient times, and after their downfall, no Mexican dynasty worth its salt failed to claim descent from these wonderful people.

Fig. 32

Like many other Post-Classic states, Toltec society, about which we understand a good deal from later records, was composed of disparate tribal elements which had come together for obscure reasons. One of these, which would appear to have been dominant, was called the Tolteca-Chichimeca. The other group went under the name Nonoalca, and according to some scholars was made up of sculptors and artisans from the old civilised regions of Puebla and the Gulf Coast, brought in to construct the monuments of Tula. The Tolteca-Chichimeca, for their part, were probably the original Nahua-speakers who founded the Toltec state. As their name implies, they were once barbarians, perhaps semi-civilised Chichimeca originating on the fringes of Mesoamerica among the Uto-Aztecans of western Mexico, for although it was said that 'they came from the interior of the plains, among the rocks', their level of culture was substantially higher than that of the 'real' Chichimeca.

Led by their semi-legendary ruler Mixcóatl ('Cloud Serpent', i.e. Milky Way), who was deified as patron of hunting after his death, the Tolteca-Chichimeca by AD 980 had entered civilised Mexico at the southern extension of the Sierra Madre Occidental, passing through what now comprises northern Jalisco and southern Zacatecas. It is no easy matter to reconstruct their history from the contradictory accounts which we have been left, but according to the generally accepted scheme of Jiménez Moreno, Mixcóatl and his people first settled at a place called Colhuacán. His son and heir was the most famous figure in all Mexican history, a very real person named Topíltzin, born in either AD 935 or 947, and later identified to the confusion of modern scholars with the Feathered Serpent, Quetzalcóatl. This king is described as being of fair skin, with long hair and a black beard.

The first event in the rule of Topíltzin Quetzalcóatl was the transfer of the Toltec capital from Colhuacán via Tulancingo to Tula, the ancient Tollan, a name signifying 'Place of the Reeds' but which to the ancients meant something like 'the city'. Some years after its founding, Tula was the scene of a terrible inner strife, for Topíltzin seems to have been a kind of priest-king dedicated to the peaceful cult of the Feathered Serpent, abhorring human sacrifice and performing all sorts of penances. His

Fig. 33. Feathered Serpent from cornice of banquette, Tula, Hidalgo. Toltec culture, Early Post-Classic Period

enemies were devotees of the fierce god Tezcatlipoca ('Smoking Mirror'), the giver and taker away of life and the patron of the warrior orders, the latter perhaps made discontented by the intellectual pacificism of their king.

As a result of this struggle for power, Topíltzin and his followers were forced to flee the city, perhaps in AD 987. Some of the most beautiful Náhuatl poetry records his unhappy downfall, a defeat laid to the door of Tezcatlipoca himself. Topíltzin and his Toltecs were said to have become slothful, the ruler having even transgressed the rules of continence. Tezcatlipoca undermines the Toltecs by various evil stratagems: coming to Topíltzin in the guise of an old man and tricking him into drinking a magic and debilitating potion; then appearing without his loin-cloth in the market-place disguised as a seller of green chili peppers, inflaming the ruler's daughter with such a desire for him that her father is forced to take him as son-in-law; next, as a warrior successfully leading a force of dwarfs and hunchbacks which had been given him in vain hope that he would be slain by the enemy; making a puppet dance for the Toltecs, causing them in their curiosity to rush forward and crush themselves to death. Even when they finally killed Tezcatlipoca by stoning, the Toltecs were unable to rid themselves of his now festering, rotted body.

At last, according to legend, Topíltzin Quetzalcóatl leaves his beloved city in exile after burning or burying all his treasures, preceded on his path by birds of precious feather. As Tula disappears from his sight:

> *Then he fixes his eyes on Tula and in that moment begins to weep :*
> *as he weeps sobbing, it is like two torrents of hail trickling down :*
> *His tears slip down his face;*
> *his tears drop by drop perforate the stones.*[4]

Plate 1

On his way trickster magicians cross his path again and again, trying to make him turn back. At last he reaches the stormy pass between the volcanoes Iztaccíhuatl and Popocatépetl, where his jugglers, buffoons, and the pages of his palace freeze to death. He continues on, his gaze directed at the shroud of the snows and eventually arrives at the shore of the Gulf of Mexico. One poem relates that there he set himself afire, decked in his quetzal plumage and turquoise mask; as his ashes rose to the sky, every kind of marvellously coloured bird wheeled overhead, and the dead king was apotheosised as the Morning Star. Another version of the tale, the one known only too well by Moctezuma II, tells us that he did not perform an act of self-immolation, but rather set off with his followers on a raft formed of serpents on a journey to the east, from which he was supposed to return some day. It is evidence of the historical core within this legend that Maya accounts speak of the arrival from the west, in the year AD 987, of a Mexican conqueror named in their tongue Kukulcán ('Feathered Serpent'), who with his companions subjugated their country. There is also ample evidence in the archaeology of Yucatan for a sea-borne Toltec invasion, successfully initiating in the late tenth century a Mexican Period.

With the sanguinary rule of the Tezcatlipoca party now dominant at Tula, the Toltec empire probably reached its greatest expansion, holding sway over most of central Mexico from coast to coast. At the height of its power, Tula is pictured in the poems as a sort of marvellous never-never land, where ears of maize were as big as *mano* stones, and red, yellow, green, blue and many other colours of cotton grew naturally. There were palaces of jade, of gold, a turquoise palace, and one made of blue-green quetzal feathers. The Toltecs were so prosperous that they heated their sweat baths with the small ears of maize. There was nothing that they could not make; wonderful potters, they 'taught the clay to lie'. Truly, they 'put their heart into their work'.

The end of Tula approached with the last ruler, Huémac. Triggered by a disastrous series of droughts, factional conflicts broke out once more, apparently between the Tolteca-Chichimeca and the Nonoalca. In 1156 or 1168 Huémac transferred his capital to Chapultepec, the hill-crowned park in what is now the western part of Mexico City, where he committed suicide. Some Tolteca-Chichimeca hung on at Tula for another 15 years, finally themselves deserting the city and moving south to the Valley of Mexico and as far as Cholula, subjugating all who lay in their way. Tula was left in ruins, with only memories of its glories. As the Náhuatl poet tells us:

> *Everywhere there meet the eye,*
> *everywhere can be seen the remains of clay vessels,*
> *of their cups, their figures,*
> *of their dolls, of their figurines,*
> *of their bracelets,*
> *everywhere are their ruins,*
> *truly the Toltecs once lived there.*[5]

The great Toltec diaspora had begun, bands of refugees wandering over highland and lowland Mexico, all claiming Tula as their homeland. Some even penetrated the Guatemala highlands, establishing new dynasties over the Mayas and imposing Mexican customs. In death, as in life, Tula remained the most potent force in Mesoamerica.

ARCHAEOLOGICAL TULA

It has been the misfortune of modern scholarship that there are not one, but many places named Tula in Mexico – a quite natural circumstance from the meaning of the name. Thus the term was indiscriminately applied to great centres like Teotihuacán and Cholula. Given this premise, the glowing descriptions appearing in the native accounts have led many an archaeologist to the erroneous conclusion that the Tula of the Toltecs must have been the admittedly magnificent Teotihuacán. In the last 35 years, however, documentary and archaeological researches have conclusively proved that the city of Topíltzin and Huémac was the Tula lying to the north-west of the Valley of Mexico, in the state of Hidalgo.

The real Tula had been so thoroughly smashed to the ground by its destroyers that it is little wonder that few were willing to grant it any importance. Its reconstruction has been for that reason extremely difficult. Placed in a defensible position on a limestone promontory, the site is surrounded by steep banks on three sides. The main group is of modest area, but mounds extend out for several miles; these have now been investigated, and indicate that Tula was a city of some size. Essentially the centre consists of a wide central plaza bordered on the east by the very badly ruined Pyramid 'C', the largest structure at Tula and as yet unexcavated; on the west by an unexplored ball court; and on the north by Pyramid 'B' and its annexes. On the north side of Pyramid 'B' is a smaller plaza, beyond which is another I-shaped ball court about 120 feet long.

Plate 53

Pyramid 'B' is the most impressive building at Tula. Built in six successive stages, in its final form this stepped pyramid-platform was fronted by a colonnaded hall, along the back of which banquettes with polychromed bas-reliefs of marching warriors were ranged. An ancient visitor would have walked through the colonnade, climbed the stairway and passed through the entrance of the temple, flanked by two stone columns in the form of Feathered Serpents, with their rattles in the air and heads on the ground. The temple itself had two rooms; the roof of

Plate 54

the outer one was supported by the heads of four colossal atlantean figures representing warriors carrying an atlatl in one hand and an incense bag in the other – perfect embodiments of Toltec artistic ideals. The rear room had four square pillars, carved on all sides with Toltec warriors adorned with the symbols of the knightly orders. There, in the sanctuary, once stood a stone altar supported by little atlantean figures. Also in the temple and in other parts of the ceremonial precinct were the peculiar

Plate 57

sculptures called 'chacmools', reclining personages bearing round dishes or receptacles for human hearts on their bellies; these were probably avatars of the Rain God.

Plate 55

Around the four sides of Pyramid 'B' were bas-reliefs symbolising the warriors orders on which the strength of the empire depended: prowling

jaguars and coyotes, and eagles eating hearts, interspersed with strange   Plate 56
composite beasts representing Quetzalcóatl.

Adjacent to this pyramid are several very spacious colonnaded halls
with sunken courts in their centres. The columns were built up of rubble
over wooden cores. Again, low banquettes extend along the walls,
which were apparently frescoed. These halls served probably for
meetings and ceremonies, rather than as palaces. In fact, two floor plans
very closely resembling the palaces of Teotihuacán have been uncovered
away from the centre of Tula, and these were certainly residences for the
rulers of the city.

On the north side of the pyramid and parallel to it is the 131-foot long
'Serpent Wall', embellished with painted friezes, the basic motif of
which is a serpent eating a human; the head has been reduced to a skull,
and the flesh has been partially stripped from the long bones.

The grim Toltec man-at-arms whose features are delineated in stone   cf. Plate 54
everywhere at Tula carried the feather-decorated atlatl in the right hand,
and a cluster of darts in the left, the Chichimec bow never appearing in
the art of civilised Mexico. Protection against enemy darts was provided
by a heavy padding of quilted cotton on the left arm and by a round
shield strapped to the back. His headgear consisted of a pillbox-shaped
hat topped by quetzal plumes and bearing on its front a bird flying
downwards. The customary nose ornament was something like a
button through the alae, and a goatee often embellished the knight's
chin. Over the chest was a highly abstract bird emblem. Either the
breechclout (*maxtli*) or the short kilt could be worn, while below leg and
ankle bands the feet were shod with backed sandals.

To turn to articles of everyday use, the very first immigrants to the site
brought with them, or adapted to their use, the red-and-buff Coyotlatelco pottery which was also current among the rabble living squalidly in
the ruins of Teotihuacán, but it gradually declined in popularity at Tula.
Soon a new kind of ware appeared, known as Mazápan, comprising
bowls whose interiors are decorated with parallel wavy or straight lines   *Fig. 34*
applied by a multiple brush; Mazápan ware appears everywhere in the
central highlands as an accompaniment of Toltec influence. Along with
it is the very distinctive Plumbate ware, one of the very few true glazed   *Fig. 35*
potteries of the pre-Spanish New World, and believed to have been
produced in kilns near the Mexican-Guatemalan border. Plumbate was

Fig. 34. *Mazápan ceramic artifacts of the Toltec culture, from Teotihuacán. a–b, Mazápan red-on-buff bowls. 1/8; c, female figurine. 1/2*

probably made to order for the Toltec taste, and one superb vessel was discovered at Tula showing the face of a bearded man between the jaws of a coyote, all completely covered with small plaques of mother-of-pearl. In clay one also finds undistinguished mould-made figurines, ladle-like incense burners with long handles, and tobacco pipes with flaring bowls and long stems embellished with undulating snakes. To date, Tula has yielded no metal of any kind, neither copper nor gold, but this need scarcely surprise us, for as yet no fine tombs, where one would expect such treasures, have been located there. On the other hand, many of the ornaments portrayed in stone are painted yellow, a colour reserved for gold in the Mexican canon.

Fig. 33

There is a singularly secular cast to Tula, for representations of the gods are rare – a state of affairs usually interpreted as the result of the encroachment of the military over the spiritual power. Curiously, the victorious Tezcatlipoca himself is absent, and the Feathered Serpent ubiquitous. Quite recognisable are representations of several deities worshipped also by the Aztecs, such as Centeocíhuatl, the Maize Goddess; Xochiquetzal, the Goddess of Love; Tlahuizcalpantecuhtli, an avatar of Quetzalcóatl as Morning Star. In line with the claim that human sacrifice was introduced in the last phase of Tula by the Tezcatlipoca faction, there are several depictions of the *cuauhxicalli*, the sacred 'eagle vessel' designed to receive human hearts, as well as a *tzompantli*, the altar decorated with skulls and crossbones on which the heads of sacrificed captives were displayed.

All the evidence points to the death of the city through sudden and overwhelming cataclysm: the ceremonial halls were burned to the ground, the Serpent Wall was toppled over, a great trench was driven into Pyramid 'B' and the huge sculptures of the sanctuary hurled in. The fury of the destruction visited on Tula makes one wonder about the hand that performed the act. The mere fact that the subsequent reoccupation of the site was by a people who used so-called 'Aztec' II pottery does not mean that the vanquishers of the capital were of the same affiliation. On the contrary the finger of accusation points most logically once more to the Chichimeca, for Tula was perilously close to their frontiers. It was just at this time that the barbarians were again pushing south into cultivated lands. When Xólotl and his band of Chichimeca passed by Tula on their way to the Valley of Mexico, they found it already in ruins and spent some days exploring its shattered walls.

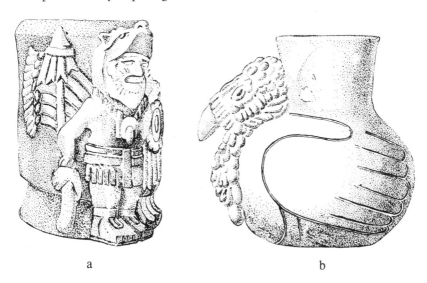

a   b

Fig. 35. Plumbate effigy jars from Teotihuacán and Tula. Toltec culture. a, bearded warrior in ocelot helmet; b, turkey effigy

LA QUEMADA – CHALCHIHUITES CULTURE

Those hardy pioneers who during Toltec times pushed up north-west along the eastern flanks of the Sierra Madre into Chichimec country, sowing their crops in what had once been barren ground, necessarily were forced to live a frontier life. As a matter of fact, this extension of cultivation into the barbarian zone had begun as far back as the Early Classic period, but it is not until the Post-Classic that one can see any major results, when a series of strongpoints was constructed. Along with these farmers also spread certain Toltec habits of pottery decoration; advanced forms of architecture, in particular the colonnaded masonry building and the platform pyramid; the ball court and the game played in it; copper bells; and perhaps the idea of masked dancers. All these traits suddenly intrude into the otherwise undistinguished farming cultures of the American South-west at about this time.

Plate 58

Plate 59

The precariousness of life along the Sierra Madre corridor is clearly manifest at the site of La Quemada, a very large hill-top fortress in the state of Zacatecas, 525 air miles north-west of Tula. To guard against Chichimec raids, a great stone wall girdles the summit, within which the bulk of the populace probably lived, farming the surrounding countryside. Outside the wall, on the lower slopes of the hill, is the ceremonial centre of La Quemada : a very odd pyramid built up of stone slabs, not truncated and lacking a stairway, along with a colonnaded hall recalling Tula. Here, though, the columns are fashioned by stacking up small, flat stones. On the summit are several smaller platform-pyramids and a complex of walled courts surrounded by rooms.

La Quemada is the most striking of a number of sites in the region sharing in a single culture, called Chalchihuites. The type site of this name, 90 miles north-west of La Quemada, is little more than another colonnaded hall on a defensible hill. Investigations have shown that the Chalchihuites culture was the intermediary between Toltec and South-western cultures like Hohokam. An analogous movement of Toltec traits took place into the south-eastern United States at the same time, probably via the peoples living on the other side of the central plateau, but little or nothing is known of the archaeology of that vast region. Suffice it to say here that most of the more spectacular aspects of the late farming cultures of the United States have an ultimately Toltec ancestry.

LATE ZAPOTEC CULTURE AT MITLA

Of all peoples of Mexico, the Zapotecs were among the most fortunate, for they had long been undisturbed in their beautiful valley by troublemakers from outside. This state of affairs was ended, however, when Monte Albán was abandoned at the close of the Classic period and a new force was spearheaded by a people infiltrating the Valley of Oaxaca from the mountainous country lying to the north-west. But more of this later.

In the early Post-Classic, a new centre of Zapotec civilisation sprang up at Mitla, about 25 miles south-west of Oaxaca City. The name is derived from the Náhuatl *Mictlan*, or 'Place of the Dead', but to the Zapotecs it was known as *Lyobaa*, 'Place of Rest'. Not very much is known of the archaeology of Mitla, but it is thought to have been begun in the poorly named 'Monte Albán IV' period, corresponding to the Toltec era; it was still in use when the Spaniards arrived.

Mitla is one of the architectural wonders of ancient Mexico – not grandiose, not a mighty city it is true – but of unparalleled beauty. Five groups of palace-like structures are scattered over the site, which is guarded by a fortified stronghold on a nearby hill. A Colonial church is built into one of these palaces and during fiestas native Zapotec ceremonies are still carried out within its precincts, side by side with Christian rites. Most remarkable among these complexes is the Group of the Columns, comprising very long masonry halls arranged on platforms around the four sides of a plaza. Here and elsewhere at Mitla long panels and entire walls are covered with geometric stonework mosaics, the intricate arabesques of which are almost entirely based on the step-and-fret motif, each piece of veneer being set into a red stucco background. From the descriptions handed down from the Colonial period, it is known that the spacious rooms of the palaces had flat roofs supported by huge horizontal beams of wood.

If we can believe the somewhat sensational but highly detailed account of pre-Spanish Mitla given us by Father Burgoa, who visited the district in the seventeenth century, this was once the residence of the High Priest of the Zapotec nation, a man so powerful that even the king bowed to his commands. Mitla's groups of buildings were apparently precincts, one for the holy man himself; one for secondary priests; one for

Plate 61

Plate 62

the Zapotec king and his court when on a visit; and one for the officials and military officers of the king. Priests carried out the ceremonies garbed in white robes and figured chasubles, amid clouds of perfumed copal incense. Hidden from vulgar eyes in an inner chamber of his palace, the High Priest ruled from a throne covered by a jaguar skin; even the king, when in his presence, took a lesser seat. Kept scrupulously clean and covered by mats, the floors were the place of repose for all occupants at night.

Burgoa asserts that gruesome sacrifices took place there continuously: numberless captives had their hearts torn out and offered to the High Priest and the Zapotec gods. Somewhere underneath Mitla was supposed to be a great secret chamber where the Zapotec kings and nobles, as well as heroes killed on the battlefront, were interred, accounting for the name of the site. The exact location of this catacomb is not known, but according to Burgoa the passage leading to it was found in his day and entered by some enterprising Spanish priests, who were soon forced by the horror of the place to scurry out again and seal it up as an abomination against God.

Now, the Spanish priests and friars were generally reliable observers and compilers of all aspects of native life. Granting some truth to Burgoa's story, how can we interpret Mitla? We know of nothing else like it in the Post-Classic, but it conforms rather accurately to the reconstruction of Classic society which has been made by many archaeologists, namely, an organised theocracy presided over by a spiritual power to whom all temporal rulers owed their allegiance. Mitla seems to have been an island in time, a survival of this older kind of social organisation into an era in which the priesthood was little more than a mouthpiece for kings who even rewrote the sacred myths for their own ends. In short, we have here one more example of Zapotec conservatism.

THE MIXTECS

'A succession of very small, rather prosperous valleys surrounded by large areas of nearby desert' is how Ignacio Bernal characterises the homeland of the Mixtec people. This is the mountainous land in western Oaxaca called the Mixteca. Miraculously, there have survived a number of codices which, through the researches of Alfonso Caso, have taken

Mixtec history back to A D 692, far beyond the range of any of the annals of other Mexican peoples.

These codices are folding deer-skin books written in late pre-Conquest days for the Mixtec nobility and containing largely the genealogies of royal houses as well as year-by-year historical accounts. Designed to be read in *boustrophedon* fashion, that is, zig-zag, from top to bottom, this writing is not truly hieroglyphic but a combination of pictographic and rebus principles, accompanied by dates of the 52-year Calendar Round. Whether this was a Mixtec invention or not, it was also adopted by the Nahua peoples grouped around the Valley of Mexico as their own. Place-names are shown by the rebus-phonetic method, and some have been identified with actual Mixtec centres in Oaxaca.

That the Mixtecs managed to bring under their sway not only all of the Mixteca proper but also most of Zapotec territory by Post-Classic times is a tribute to their statecraft. This was of a simple sort, quite familiar in European history, namely for an aggressive prince to marry into the royal line of a coveted town if he was unable to take it by force; polygamy made this strategy fairly common. Often, if he actually subdued the enemy by force of arms, he would further consolidate his rule by a judicious marriage with a native princess. Extensive intermarriage eventually resulted in the Mixtec aristocracy being one family, under a single dynastic house. As with royalty of Egypt, Hawaii, and Peru, policy considerations led even to brother-sister marriage.

Claiming descent from the Feathered Serpent, they said that their ancestors were born from trees in a certain part of the upper Mixteca. By the Late Classic period, the leading power in the Mixteca was a town called Mountain that Opens; overthrown in A D 859 or 875, its rulers were sacrificed. We now see the establishment of the First Dynasty of Tilantongo, which jointly ruled the valleys with a place called Xipe Bundle, until it too fell.

In the Second Dynasty of Tilantongo, the codices have much to tell about a person named 8 Deer (like most Mexicans, the Mixtecs took one of their names from the day of their birth). Born in A D 1011, his eventful life continued until 1063, during which time the Mixtecs were clearly under powerful Toltec influence. As a boy he accompanied the war parties of his father, the king; he himself soon became a mighty war

Fig. 36

leader, subduing town after town. In 1045, 8 Deer made a journey to Tula, where he was invested with the Toltec nose button by either the Toltec king himself, a man called 4 Jaguar, or by his chief priest 8 Death; this probably marks his accession to the throne, the ruler of the Toltec capital fulfilling the same function as the pope who crowned the Holy Roman emperor.

We follow in the books the machinations of 8 Deer, as he brings all of the rival statelets under his sway: marrying no less than five times, all his wives were princesses of other towns, some of whose families he had subjected to the sacrificial knife. When he was 52 years old, he made the mistake of attacking the native town of the last of his wives, and he himself was captured, suffering the usual fate.

The most mysterious event in his life is the record of his visit to the king of a place called Hill of the Sun, believed by some to be in southern Puebla near Teotitlán del Camino; not only 8 Deer, but the lord of Tula

Fig. 36. Scenes from the life of the Mixtec king, 8 Deer, from the Codex Nuttall. Right, 8 Deer has his nose pierced for a special ornament in the year A D 1045. Centre, 8 Deer goes to war. Left, town 'Curassow Hill' conquered by 8 Deer. 3/4

paid homage to this man. Who was he? Was there some empire more powerful than the Toltec about which we know nothing? This is one of the great unsolved puzzles of Mexican archaeology.

By approximately A D 1350 the Mixtecs began to infiltrate even the Valley of Oaxaca by the usual method of state marriage, Mixtec royal brides insisting on bringing their own retinues to the Zapotec court. By the time the Spaniards arrived, practically all Zapotec sites were occupied by the Mixtecs. Of their great wealth and high artistry, for they were the finest goldsmiths and workers in turquoise mosaic in Mexico, the fantastic treasure from Tomb 7 at Monte Albán is eloquent testimony. Here, in an older Monte Albán III-B tomb, the Mixtecs laid the remains of one of their kings and the bodies of his slaughtered servants, some time in the mid-fourteenth century. Accompanying the ruler were magnificent objects of gold, cast in the lost-wax process, and silver; turquoise mosaics; necklaces of rock crystal, amber, jet, and coral;

Plate 63

Plate 64

thousands of pearls, one as big as a pigeon's egg; and sections of jaguar bone carved with historic and mythological scenes. Not only to the south, but as far north as Cholula, Mixtec artistic influence was felt, resulting in the hybrid Mixteca-Puebla style which produced some of the finest manuscripts, sculpture, pottery, and turquoise mosaics of latter-day Mexico.

Neither the Zapotecs, nor the Mixtecs, although marked for conquest in its aggressive plans, were ever completely vanquished by the Aztec state. Proud of their own languages and rich cultural backgrounds, they united successfully against the intruder and thus avoided the fate of so many other once independent nations of Post-Classic Mexico.

CHAPTER VIII

The Post-Classic Period:
The Aztec Empire

The beginnings of the Aztec nation were so humble and obscure that their rise to supremacy over most of Mexico in the space of a few hundred years seems almost miraculous. It is somehow inconceivable that the magnificent civilisation witnessed and destroyed by the Spaniards could have been created by a people who were not many generations removed from the most abject barbarism, but such was the case. It is only through an understanding of this fact, namely the tribal roots of the Aztec state, that these extraordinary people can really be comprehended.

PEOPLES AND POLITICS IN THE VALLEY OF MEXICO

When any great state collapses, it is inevitable that unless there is another comparable force to take its place, conditions of anarchy will ensue. This is exactly what happened in the Valley of Mexico and surrounding regions in the wake of Tula's destruction in the twelfth century. Refugees from this centre of Toltec civilisation managed to establish themselves in the southern half of the Valley, particularly at the towns of Colhuacán and Xico, both of which became important citadels transmitting the higher culture of their predecessors to the savage groups who were then streaming into the northern half. Among the latter were the band of Chichimeca under their chief Xólotl, arriving in the Valley by 1244 and settling at Tenayuca; the Acolhua, who founded Coatlínchan around the year 1260; the Otomí at Xaltocan by about 1250; and the powerful Tepanecs, who in 1230 took over the older town of Atzcapotzalco, which it will be remembered was originally founded by Teotihuacán refugees. There is no question that all of these with the exception of the Otomí were speakers of Náhuatl, now the dominant tongue of central Mexico. Thus, by the thirteenth century, all over the Valley there had sprung up a group of modestly sized city states, those in the north

Fig. 38

founded by Chichimec upstarts eager to learn from the Toltecs in the south.

It was inevitable that a jockeying for power among these rivals would take place, and it was the northern centres which grew at the expense of the southern. Into this uneasy political situation stepped the last barbaric tribe to arrive in the Valley of Mexico, the Aztecs, the 'people whose face nobody knows'. They said that they came from a place called 'Aztlán' in the west of Mexico, believed by some authorities to be in the state of Nayarit, and had wandered about guided by the image of their tribal god, Huitzilopochtli ('Hummingbird-on-the-left'), who was borne on the shoulders of four priests. Apparently they knew the art of cultivation and wore agave fibre clothing, but had no political leaders higher than clan and tribal chieftains. It is fitting that Huitzilopochtli was a war god and a representative of the sun, for the Aztecs were extremely adept at military matters, and among the best and fiercest warriors ever seen in Mexico. They were also among the most bloodthirsty, for their deity demanded quantities of human hearts extracted from captive warriors, and it was not long before they had a very evil reputation for savagery among their more civilised neighbours.

It was not only their unpleasant habits which failed to endear them, but also the fact that they were outright intruders. All the land in the Valley was already occupied by civilised peoples, who looked with suspicion upon these Aztecs, who were little more than squatters, continually occupying territory that did not belong to them and continually being kicked out. It is a wonder that they were ever tolerated since, women being scarce as among all immigrant groups, they took to raiding other peoples for their wives. The cultivated citizens of Colhuacán finally allowed them to live a degraded existence, working the lands of their masters as serfs, and supplementing their diet with snakes and other vermin. In 1323, however, the Aztecs repaid the kindness of their overlords, who had given their chief a Colhuacán princess as bride, by sacrificing the young lady with the hope that she would become a war goddess. Colhuacán retaliated by expelling these repulsive savages from their territory.

We next see the Aztecs following a hand-to-mouth existence in the marshes of the great lake. On they wandered, loved by none, until they reached some swampy, unoccupied islands, covered by rushes, near the western shore; it was claimed that there the tribal prophecy, to build a city where an eagle was seen sitting on a cactus, holding a snake in its mouth, was fulfilled. By 1344 or 1345, the tribe was split in two, one group under their chief, *Tenoch*, founding the southern capital, Tenochtitlán, and the other settling Tlatelolco in the north. Eventually, as the swamps were drained and brought under cultivation, the islands became one, with two cities and two governments, a state of affairs not to last very long.

Fig. 38

The year 1367 marks the turning point of Aztec fortunes. It was then that the Aztecs began to serve as mercenaries for the mightiest power on the mainland, the expanding Tepanec kingdom of Atzcapotzalco, ruled by the unusually able Tezozómoc. One after another the city states of the Valley of Mexico fell to the joint forces of Tezozómoc and his allies; sharing in the resulting loot, the Aztecs were also taken under Tepanec protection, Tezozómoc giving them their first king, Acama- pichtli. At the same time, and in fact probably beginning as far back as their serfdom under Colhuacán, the Aztecs were taking on much of the culture that was the heritage of all the nations of the Valley from their Toltec predecessors. Much of this was learned from the mighty Tepanecs themselves, particularly the techniques of statecraft and empire-building so successfully indulged in by Tezozómoc. Already the small island kingdom of the Aztecs was prepared to exercise its strength on the mainland.

THE CONSOLIDATION OF AZTEC POWER

The chance came in 1426, when the aged Tezozómoc was succeeded as Tepanec king by his son Maxtlatzin, known to the Aztecs as 'Tyrant Maxtla' and an implacable enemy of the growing power of Tenochtit- lán. By crude threats and other pressures, Maxtlatzin attempted to rid himself of the 'Aztec problem'; and in the middle of the crisis, the third Aztec king died. Itzcóatl, who assumed the Aztec rulership in 1427, was a man of strong mettle. More important, he had in his chief adviser, the great Tlacaélel, one of the most remarkable men ever produced by the Mexicans. The two of them decided to fight, with the result that by the next year the Tepanecs had been totally crushed and Azcapotzalco was in ruins. This great battle, for ever glorious to the Aztecs, left them the greatest state in Mexico.

In their triumph, the Aztec administration turned to questions of internal polity, especially under Tlacaélel, who remained a kind of grand vizier to the Aztec throne through three reigns, dying in 1475 or 1480. Tlacaélel conceived of and implemented a series of reforms that completely altered Mexican life. The basic reform related to the Aztec conception of themselves and their destiny; for this, it was necessary to rewrite history, and so Tlacaélel did, by having all of the books of conquered peoples burned since these would have failed to mention Aztec glories. Under his aegis, the Aztecs acquired a mystic-visionary view of themselves as the chosen people, the true heirs of the Toltec tradition, who would fight wars and gain captives so as to keep the fiery sun moving across the sky.

This sun, represented by the fierce god Huitzilopochtli, needed the hearts of enemy warriors; during the reign of Moctezuma I (1440–68), Tlacaélel had the so-called 'Flowery War' instituted. Under this, Tenochtitlán entered into a Triple Alliance with the old Acolhua state of Texcoco (on the other side of the lake) and the dummy state of Tlacopan in a permanent struggle against the Náhuatl-speaking states of Tlaxcala and Huexotzingo. The object on both sides was purely to gain captives for sacrifice.

Besides inventing the idea of Aztec 'grandeur', the glorification of the Aztec past, other reforms relating to the political-juridical and economic administrations were also carried out under Tlacaélel. The new system was successfully tested during a disastrous two-year famine which occurred under Moctezuma I, and from which this extraordinary people emerged more confident than ever in their divine mission.

Given these conditions, it is little surprise that the Aztecs soon embarked with their allies on an ambitious programme of conquest. The elder Moctezuma began the expansion, taking over the Huasteca, much of the land around Mount Orizaba, and rampaging down even into the Mixteca. Axayácatl (1469–81) subdued neighbouring Tlatelolco on trumped-up charges and substituted a military government for what had once been an independent administration; he was less successful with the Tarascan kingdom of Michoacan, for these powerful people were already equipped with copper weapons and turned the invaders back. Greatest of all the empire-builders was Ahuítzotl (1486–1502), who succeeded the weak and vacillating Tizoc as sixth king. This mighty

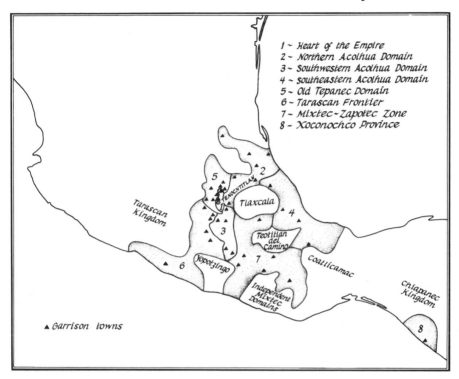

1 ~ *Heart of the Empire*
2 ~ *Northern Acolhua Domain*
3 ~ *Southwestern Acolhua Domain*
4 ~ *Southeastern Acolhua Domain*
5 ~ *Old Tepanec Domain*
6 ~ *Tarascan Frontier*
7 ~ *Mixtec-Zapotec Zone*
8 ~ *Xoconochco Province*

Tarascan Kingdom

TENOCHTITLAN

Tlaxcala

Teotitlan del Camino

Yopotzingo

Coatlicamac

Independent Mixtec Domains

Chiapanec Kingdom

▲ *Garrison towns*

Fig. 37. Extent of the Aztec Empire in 1520. The provinces into which the Aztec domains were organised are indicated

warrior conquered lands all the way to the Guatemalan border and brought under Aztec rule most of central Mexico. Probably for the first time since the downfall of Tula, there was in Mexico a single empire as great as, or greater than, that of the Toltecs. Ahuítzotl was a man of great energy; among the projects completed in his reign were the Great Temple of Tenochtitlán, for the dedication of which no less than 20,000 captives gained in the 'Flowery War' were sacrificed, and the construction of an aqueduct to bring water from Coyoacán to the island capital.

A more tragic figure in history than his successor, Moctezuma II (1502–20), would be hard to imagine. It was his misfortune to be a very complex person, not the kind of single-minded militarist that is so well typified by Ahuítzotl. Instead of delighting in war, he was given to meditation in his place of retreat, the 'Black House' – in fact, he was more of a philosopher king, along the lines of Hadrian. Like that Roman emperor, he also maintained a shrine in the capital where all of the gods of captured nations were kept, for he was interested in foreign religions. It is certain that Moctezuma II was deeply imbued with Toltec traditions. This was the cause of his downfall, for when Cortés arrived in 1519, the Aztec emperor was paralysed by the realisation that this strange, bearded foreigner was Quetzalcóatl himself, returned with his Toltecs from the east as the ancient books had said he would, to destroy the Mexican peoples. All of his disastrous inaction in the face of the Spanish threat, his willingness to put himself in the hands of Cortés, was brought about by this dedication to the old Toltec philosophy. It was his destiny, foretold by a series of magical portents, to preside over the total destruction of Mexican civilisation.

THE AZTECS IN 1519

Let the soldier Bernal Díaz, who was with Hernán Cortés when the Spaniards first approached the island capital of Tenochtitlán on 8th November 1519, tell us his impressions of his first glimpse of the Aztec citadel:

> During the morning, we arrived at a broad causeway and continued our march towards Iztapalapa, and when we saw so many cities and villages built in the water and other great towns on dry land and that straight and level Causeway going towards Mexico, we were amazed and said that it was like the enchantments they tell of in the legend of Amadis, on account of the great towers and cues and buildings rising from the water, and all built of masonry. And some of our soldiers asked whether the things that we saw were not a dream.[6]

Fig. 38

The island was connected to the mainland by three causeways, 'each as broad as a horseman's lance', says Cortés, running north to Tepeyac, west to Tlacopan, and south to Coyoacán. These were broken at intervals by openings through which canoes could pass, and spanned by

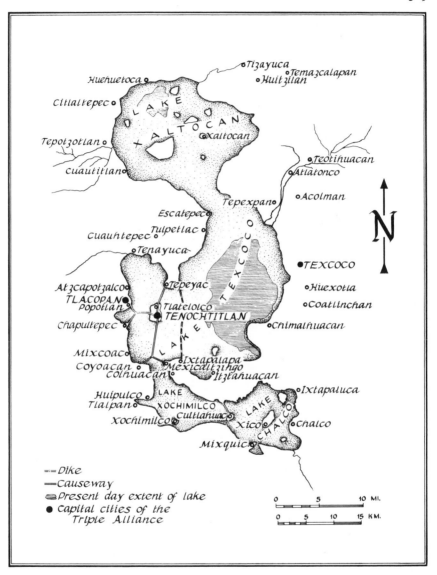

Fig. 38. The Valley of Mexico in Aztec times

removable bridges, thus serving a defensive purpose; moreover, access to the city by the enemy was barred by manned gatehouses. Across the western causeway ran a great masonry aqueduct carrying water to Tenochtitlán from the spring at Chapultepec, the flow being 'as thick as a man's body'.

The Spanish conquerors called the Aztec capital another Venice, and they should have known, for many of them had actually been to that place. With a total area of about 20 square miles, the city (meaning by this Tenochtitlán and its satellite Tlatelolco) was laid out on a grid, according to a fragmentary sixteenth-century map of one section. Running north and south were long canals thronged with canoe traffic and each bordered by a lane; larger canals cut there at angles. Between these watery 'streets' were arranged in regular fashion rectangular plots of land with their houses. In effect, this was a *chinampa* city.

A brief description of *chinampa* cultivation, mentioned in Chapter I, will not be out of place here. The technique is well known, for it is still

Plate 2

used in the Xochimilco zone to the south of Mexico City. The first settlers on the island constructed canals in their marshy habitat by cutting layers of thick water vegetation from the surface and piling them up like mats to make their plots; from the bottom of the canals they spread mud over these green 'rafts', which were thoroughly anchored by planting willows all around. On this highly fertile plot all sorts of crops were raised by the most careful and loving hand cultivation. This is why Cortés states that half the houses in the capital were built up 'on the lake', and how swampy islands became united. Those houses on newly made *chinampas* were necessarily of light cane and thatch; on drier parts of the island, more substantial dwellings of stone and mortar were possible, some of two stories with flower-filled inner patios and gardens. Communication across the 'streets' was by planks laid over the canals.

The greatest problem faced by the inhabitants was the saltiness of the lake, at least in its eastern part. With no outlet, during floods those nitrous waters inundated and ruined the *chinampas*. To prevent this, the Texcocan king Nezahualcóyotl bountifully constructed a ten-mile-long dyke to seal off a spring-fed, freshwater lagoon for Tenochtitlán.

With its willows, green gardens, numerous flowers, and canals bustling with canoes, Tenochtitlán must have been of impressive beauty, as the Náhuatl poem suggests:

The city is spread out in circles of jade,
radiating flashes of light like quetzal plumes,
Beside it the lords are borne in boats:
over them extends a flowery mist.[7]

It is extraordinarily difficult to estimate the population of the capital in 1519. Many early sources say that there were about 60,000 houses, but none say how many persons there were. The data which we have, however flimsy, suggest that Tenochtitlán (with Tlatelolco) had from 200,000 to 300,000 inhabitants when Cortés marched in, five times the size of the contemporary London of Henry VIII. Quite a number of other cities of central Mexico, such as Texcoco, also had very large populations; all of Mexico between the Isthmus of Tehuantepec and the Chichimec frontier had about 11 million inhabitants, most of whom were under Aztec domination.

At the centre of Tenochtitlán, the focal point of all the main highways which led in from the mainland, was the administrative and religious heart of the empire. Surrounded by a 'Snake Wall' was the Sacred Precinct, a paved area dominated by the 100-foot-high double temple-pyramid, the Temple of Huitzilopochtli and Tlaloc, its twin stairways reddened with the blood of sacrificed captives. Other temples were dedicated to the cults of Tezcatlipoca and Xipe Totec. A gruesome reminder of the purpose of the never-ending 'Flowery War' was the *tzompantli*, or skull rack, on which were skewered for public exhibition tens of thousands of human heads. Having hardly more pleasant associations was a very large ball court, in which Moctezuma II played and lost a game to the king of Texcoco on the truth of the latter's prediction that the former's kingdom would fall. The magnificent palaces of the Aztec royal line surrounded the Sacred Precinct.

Both in Tenochtitlán and in Tlatelolco proper were great market-places, very close to the main temples. The latter market was described by Bernal Díaz in superlative terms; some of the Spanish soldiers who had been in Rome and Constantinople claimed that it was larger than any there. Every product had its own place, the shops being arranged along the streets. So many persons came to buy and sell in the daily markets held there that there were market inspectors appointed by the king to check the honesty of transactions and to regulate prices. As for 'money',

Fig. 39

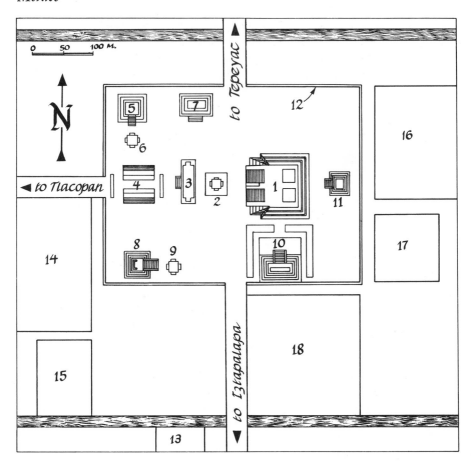

Fig. 39. The centre of Tenochtitlán in 1520, with main streets and canals. 1. Great Temple of Tlaloc and Huitzilopochtli. 2. Platform for stone of Tizoc. 3. Tzompantli *(skull rack). 4. Ball court. 5. 'Eagle House' of the Sun Temple. 6. Platform of the 'Eagle House', base for Calendar Stone. 7. Snake Temple. 8. Temple of Xipe Totec, God of Spring. 9. Platform for gladiatorial stone. 10. Temple of Tezcatlipoca. 11. Temple of Colhuacán, the former temple of Huitzilopochtli. 12. Snake Wall, enclosing the sacred precinct. 13. 'Black House' of the Temple of Coatlícue. 14. Palace of Moctezuma I (1440–69). 15. 'House of the Songs'. 16. Palace of Axayácatl (1469–81). 17. Royal Aviary. 18. Palace of Moctezuma II (1502–20)*

cacao beans (which sometimes were counterfeited), cotton cloaks, and transparent quills filled with gold dust served that purpose. Befitting its role as the commercial centre of an empire, in the Great Market of Tlatelolco one could buy luxury products of gold, silver, jade, turquoise, or feathers; clothing of all sorts; foods both cooked and unprepared; pottery, the most esteemed being lovely polychrome dishes and cups from Cholula; chocolate and vanilla; carpenter's tools of copper; cane cigarettes, tobacco pipes, and aromatic cigars; and slaves, human cattle brought in by dealers from the slave centre of Atzcapotzalco and exhibited in wooden cages. The market people had the obligation to furnish war provisions to the state, mainly maize in forms that would not spoil on long marches.

Plate 71

An empire, a tremendous state in place of what had been less than two centuries before but a band of miserable wretches leading a tribal existence – small wonder that the structure of Aztec society was still in a state of transition in 1519. And yet it is utterly false to assert that the Aztecs when first seen by the Spaniards were on the clan level of organisation, without any kind of political power greater than that enjoyed by, say, an Iroquois chief. On the other hand, relics of a more simple kind of organisation of human affairs certainly persisted in the administration of the empire.

There were four basic social groups in Aztec Mexico. At the top of the ladder were the noblemen or *pilli*, who all belonged to the royal house, 'precious feathers from the wings of past kings', as one source puts it. It was from their ranks that the imperial administrators were drawn; these had the use of lands belonging to their office and also owned private lands.

The vast bulk of the population were commoners, *macehualli*, organised into *calpulli*, or clans, of which there were about twenty in the capital. All members of a *calpulli* claimed descent from a common ancestor and worked lands which could not be alienated from their group; each family with its plot maintained rights over it as long as it did not lie unused for over two years at a time. As a landholding corporation, each *calpulli* lived in its own ward in the city; Tenochtitlán itself was divided into four great quarters, and every quarter into its constituent *calpulli*, every *calpulli* into *tlaxilacalli*, or streets. Quite obviously, this was an ideal system for administrative control of a large population. The individual *calpulli* had its own temple and some of the more high-ranking of them had schools for the military education of their youth.

At the bottom of the social scale were the bondsmen (*mayeque*), who tilled the estates of the noblemen as serfs; the majority of them would seem to have been the original owners of lands seized from them by Aztec conquest and handed over to be held in severalty by the 'principals'. Another humble group consisted of the *tamime*, porters who hired themselves out to the professional merchants and who may have been semi-civilised Chichimecs from the frontier. Slaves as a group were not important; their membership was drawn from captives and from those who had sold themselves to relieve debts. They were well treated and could not be inherited.

In spite of the presence of clans among the Aztecs, there was nothing in the least bit egalitarian about their society. Everybody was ranked according to their contiguity to the ancestral founders of the *calpulli*, quarter, or nation. As a consequence, there were aristocratic families within the *calpulli* who directed its actions and aristocratic *calpulli* within each quarter. The highest ranking *calpulli* of the greatest quarter in Tenochtitlán was that of the nobility, who claimed descent on the distaff side from Quetzalcóatl; within it, the greatest lineage was that of the royal family. A regular system of tribute offering of one third of the products of the soil ensured the maintenance of the clan aristocracies and the nobility, each élite group drawing its support from the units below it.

We see here, then, a society evolved from a more or less primitive organisation in which all lands were originally held by the clans and over which there was no higher authority than clan chiefs, into a fully fledged state with the appearance of a privileged class holding authority by virtue of its wealth drawn from private estates worked by a new lower class, the serfs. Given time, the clans would have certainly declined to total insignificance.

Two other groups were also to a certain degree operating outside the old clan system. Warriors distinguished on the field of battle were often given their own lands and relieved from the necessity of supplying tribute. The *pochteca* were the long-distance traders engaged in the obtaining of exotic products for the royal palace. Travelling into foreign territories hundreds of miles from the capital, they gathered military intelligence as well as needed goods for the crown, in special ports of trade. Like the businessmen'spies of modern days, they often were the vanguard for the Aztec take'over of another nation, acting sometimes as *agents'provocateurs*. While organised into their own *calpulli,* with their own god, they could render tribute to the palace in luxury goods rather than the produce of their lands, and grew rich and powerful as a consequence – perhaps the nucleus of a crystallising merchant class.

Moctezuma II, the emperor, was the greatest landowner of all. Among the Aztecs, the king was elected from the royal lineage by a council composed of the nobles, chief priests, and top war officers; at the same time, the four principal lords who were to act as his executive arm were also chosen. On his installation, the new king was taken by the chief priests to pay homage at the temple of the national god, Huitzilopochtli; while he censed the sacred image, the masses of citizens waited expectantly below, in a din caused by the blowing of shell trumpets. After four days of meditation and fasting in the temple, he was escorted to his palace. To his coronation banquet came even the kings of distant lands, like the rulers of the Tarascan kingdom, the king of the Totonacs, and great personages from as far as Tehuantepec.

Fig. 39

The Aztec king was in every sense an absolute ruler, although advised and sometimes guided by his councillors, particularly by the man who filled the office of *Cihuacóatl* ('Female Snake'), the grand vizier. The descriptions of the Spaniards make it clear that the ruler was semi'divine. Even great lords who entered into his presence approached in plain garments, heads bowed, without looking on his face. Everywhere he went, he was borne on the shoulders of noblemen in a litter covered with precious feathers. If he walked, nobles swept the way and covered the ground with cloths so that his feet would not touch the ground. When Moctezuma ate, he was shielded from onlookers by a gilt screen. No less than several hundred dishes were offered at each meal for his choosing by young maidens; during his repast he was entertained by buffoons, dwarfs, juggler, and tumblers.

Moctezuma's gardens and pleasure palaces amazed the Spaniards. The royal aviary had ten large rooms with pools of salt and fresh water, housing birds of both lake and sea, above which were galleries bordered by hanging gardens for the imperial promenade. Another building was the royal zoo, staffed by trained veterinarians, in which were exhibited in cages animals from all parts of his realm – jaguars from the lowlands, pumas from the mountains, foxes, and so forth, making an unearthly clamour with their roars and howls. Carefully tended by servants, many kinds of deformed persons and monstrosities inhabited his private side-show, each with his own room.

Less frivolous activities of the royal household included separate courts of justice for noblemen (and warriors) and for commoners; the overseeing by stewards of the palace storehouse; the maintenance of the state arsenal, officers' quarters, and the military academy; and the management of the empire-wide tribute system.

All of these state functions, and the Aztec economy itself, ultimately rested on the agricultural base of the Mexican peoples – the farming of maize, beans, squash, tomatoes, amaranth, sage, and many other cultigens. Thousands of canoes daily crowded the great lake, bearing these products to the capital either as direct tribute or as merchandise to be traded for craft items and other necessities in the market-places. A tremendous surplus for the use of the city was extracted from the rich *chinampas* fringing the shallow lake and from irrigated fields near by.

Plate 2

But the main goal of the Aztec state was war. Every able-bodied man was expected to bear arms, even the priests and the merchants, the latter fighting in their own units while ostensibly on trading expeditions. To the Aztecs, there was no activity more glorious than to furnish captives or to die oneself for Huitzilopochtli:

> *The battlefield is the place:*
> *where one toasts the divine liquor in war,*
> *where are stained red the divine eagles,*
> *where the jaguars howl,*
> *where all kinds of precious stones rain from ornaments,*
> *where wave headdresses rich with fine plumes,*
> *where princes are smashed to bits.*[8]

In the rich imagery of Náhuatl song, the blood-stained battlefield was described as an immense plain covered by flowers, and lucky he who perished on it:

> *There is nothing like death in war,*
> *nothing like the flowery death*

so precious to Him who gives life:
far off I see it: my heart yearns for it! [9]

Aztec weapons were the terrible sword-club, with side grooves set with
razor-sharp obsidian blades; spears, the heads of which were also set
with blades; and barbed and fletched darts hurled from the atlatl. The
Aztec warrior was gorgeously arrayed in costumes of jaguar skins or suits
covered with eagle feathers, symbolising the knightly orders; for defence
he sometimes was clad in a quilted cotton tunic and always carried a
round shield, often magnificently decorated with coloured designs in
feathers. Acting as mercenaries, fierce Otomí tribesmen accompanied
the army as bowmen.

War strategy included the gathering of intelligence and compilation
of maps. On the field of battle, the ranks of the army were arranged by
generals. Attacks were spear-headed by an élite corps of veteran warriors,
followed by the bulk of the army, to the sound of shell trumpets blown
by priests. The idea was not only to destroy the enemy town but also to
isolate and capture as many of the enemy as possible for transport to the
rear and eventual sacrifice in the capital.

Nations which had fallen to Aztec arms and those of their allies in the
Triple Alliance were speedily organised as tribute-rendering provinces Fig. 37
of the empire. Military governors in Aztec garrisons ensured that such
tribute, which was very heavy indeed, was paid promptly and on fixed
dates. It is fortunate that the tribute list in Moctezuma's state archives has Plate 72
survived in the form of copies, for the Spaniards were also interested in
what they could extract from the old Aztec provinces. Incredible as it
may seem, each year Tenochtitlán received from all parts of the empire
7,000 tons of maize and 4,000 tons each of beans, sage seed, and grain
amaranth, and no less than two million cotton cloaks, as well as war
costumes, shields, feather headdresses, and luxury products like amber
unobtainable in the central highlands. Certainly some of this loot,
especially the cloaks, was farmed out by the royal treasury to the *pochteca*
as barter goods to carry to distant ports of trade. But a good deal of the
tribute acted as the main financial support of the state edifice, since in an
essentially moneyless economy state servants had to be paid in goods and
land, and artisans had to receive something for the fine products which
they supplied to the palace.

Not unsurprisingly, many of the provinces held under such a heavy yoke reacted to the arrival of Cortés by welcoming the invaders from across the sea as a miraculous delivery from a rule which seemed to them a tyranny.

Aztec mythology and religious organisation are so incredibly complex that little justice can be given them in the space of this chapter. The Aztec concept of the supernatural world was a result of the reconciliation by mystic intellectuals of the tribal gods of their own people to the far richer cosmogony of the older civilisations of Mexico, welding both into a single great system. The bewildering multiplicity of Mexican gods were to these thinkers but embodiments of one cosmic principle of duality, male and female, darkness and light, life and death, as personified by the struggle of Quetzalcóatl and Tezcatlipoca, or by Quetzalcóatl and the Death God. It was believed that the world had

Plate 73

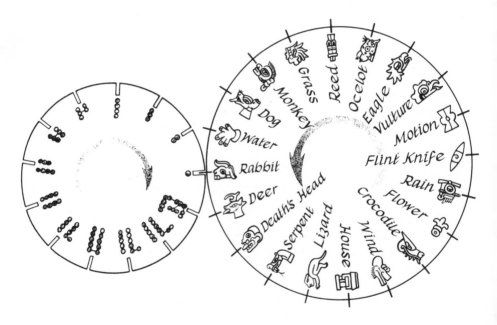

Fig. 40. Schematic representation of the tonalpohualli *or 260-day period of the Aztecs. The twenty named days intermesh with the numbers one to 13*

gone through four cosmic ages or Suns (like the Hindu *kalpas*), each destroyed by a cataclysm; the present was the fifth age, to be extinguished by earthquakes.

Added to the nature gods and culture heroes already familiar to us in Teotihuacán and Tula were the concepts codified by Tlacaélel, comprising the official state cult of the Aztecs. Huitzilopochtli, the terrible warrior god of the Sun, was the miraculous result of the impregnation of his mother, Coatlícue ('Serpent-Skirt'), by a ball of feathers as she was sweeping one day. As she gave birth, her other children, the Four Hundred Gods, killed her by cutting off her head.

Plate 66

All of these deities were thought of as being multiple, that is simultaneously appearing in quadruple form, each constituent placed at one of the four directions of the universe and associated with a particular colour, so that there were white, black, red, and blue Tezcatlipocas, for instance.

The cults were presided over by a celibate clergy. Every priest had been to a seminary at which he was instructed in the complicated ritual which he was expected to carry out daily. Their long, unkempt hair clotted with blood, their ears and members shredded from self-mutilations effected with agave thorns and sting-ray spines, smelling of death and putrefaction, they must have been awesome spokesmen for the Aztec gods.

The daily life of all Aztecs was bound up with the ceremonies dictated by the machine-like workings of their calendar. The Almanac Year (*tonalpohualli*) of 260 days was the result of the intermeshing of twenty days (given names like Crocodile, Wind, House, Lizard, etc.) with the numbers one to thirteen, expressed in their books by dots only. To all individuals, each day in the *tonalpohualli* brought good or evil tidings in accordance with the prognostications of the priests; but the bad effects could be mitigated, so that if a child was born on an unfavourable day, his naming ceremony could be postponed to a better one. For each of the thirteen 'weeks' there were special rites and presiding gods, as well as gods for every day and even for the hours of day and night.

Fig. 40

The Solar Year was made up of 18 named months of 20 days each, with an unlucky and highly dangerous period of five extra days before the commencement of the next year. Again, every month had its own special ceremonies in which all of the citizens of the capital participated; given the nature of this kind of cycle, it is hardly surprising that the months were closely correlated with the agricultural year. Such Solar Years were named after one of the four possible day names of the Almanac Year which could fall on the last day of the eighteenth month along with its accompanying numerical coefficient.

All this was recorded in folding-screen books of deer skin or agave paper, kept in the temples by the priests. The state archives also included economic accounts and, possibly, historical works. Curiously, no truly Aztec codices have survived the Conquest; the finest Post-Classic books which we have were painted in a place that with some confidence can be indicated as Cholula. But about the Aztec script we have some knowledge, for it definitely was of the rebus, 'puzzle-writing' sort; most frequently appearing were place-names, recorded so as to take advantage of common Náhuatl words: thus, the town 'Atlan' was written by combining pictographs of water (*atl*) and teeth (*tlantli*). Numbers up to 19 were expressed by dots, 20 by a flag, 400 by something like a pine tree, 8,000 by a pouch for holding copal incense – that is, the system was vigesimal, increasing in multiples of twenty.

The ritual round must have provided year-long excitement and meaning to the life of the ordinary citizen of Tenochtitlán, with feasts, decoration of the idols, and dances and songs to the accompaniment of two-toned slit drums, upright drums, conch-shell trumpets, rattles, and flutes. Homage to the gods prescribed individual penances and burning of blood-spattered paper, burning of perfumed copal incense, and, most dramatically, immolation of thousands of human captives yearly. The victims themselves considered it a glorious death to be seized by the priests and stretched on their backs over a stone on the temple summit, an incision made in the chest with a flint knife, the heart ripped out and placed in the *cuauhxicalli*, or 'Eagle Vase', to be burned for the consumption of the gods. Quickly the head was cut from the corpse, and the body flayed. Priests and those doing penance garbed themselves in the victim's skin, which was worn for twenty days at the end of which the god-impersonator (for they then represented Xipe, the Flayed One) 'stank like a dead dog', as one source tells us.

Most famous among the Aztec sacrifices was that of the young captive annually chosen to impersonate the god Tezcatlipoca. For one year he

Plates 73, 74

Plate 70

lived a life of honour, worshipped literally as the embodiment of the deity; towards the end, he was given four beautiful maidens as his mistresses. Finally, he left them sadly, mounted the steps of the temple, smashing one by one the clay flutes on which he had played in his brief moment of glory, then was flung on his back so that the flint dagger might be plunged into his breast. Most horrible of Aztec practices was the mass sacrifice of small children on mountain tops to bring rain at the end of the dry season, in propitiation of Tlaloc; it was said that the more they cried, the more the Rain God was pleased.

Aztec art and architecture were primarily ecclesiastical, rather than secular in nature. The levelling of the Sacred Precinct of Tenochtitlán by the Spaniards for their own administrative buildings and cathedral destroyed all but the foundations of the major Aztec temples, but some idea can be gained of their magnificence by those that remain elsewhere in the Valley of Mexico, such as the huge double temple at Tenayuca, or the wonderful rock-carved sanctuary at Malinalco, circular and therefore certainly sacred to Quetzalcóatl. To some eyes, Aztec sculpture may be repulsive and there is no doubt that the monumental figures of gods like Coatlícue may be terrifying, but there is no denying their awesome power. But power is also reflected in the more 'realistic' works such as the seated stone figure of Xochipilli ('Prince of Flowers'), the god of love and summertime, which continue traditions of workmanship perfected by the Toltecs. Or, in the same vein, the lovely sculptured drums from Malinalco, one of which recalls the Náhuatl war song:

Plate 65

Plate 66

Plate 68

Plate 69

> *The earth shakes: the Mexica [Aztec] begins his song:*
> *He makes the Eagles and Jaguars dance with him!*
> *Come to see the Huexotzinca:*
> *On the dais of the Eagle he shouts out,*
> *Loudly cries the Mexica.*[10]

Aztec artisans in Tenochtitlán were arranged in an approximation of guilds and were famous for their fine work in feather mosaics; but they were hardly rivals to the great craftsmen of the Cholula area, who under influence from the Mixtecs in the south and Aztecs in the north produced the magnificent Mixteca-Puebla style. Moctezuma himself would eat only from cups and plates of Cholula ware, and it is sure that

Plate 71

much of the gold work as well as practically all of the fine masks and other ceremonial paraphernalia of wood encrusted with turquoise mosaic were also manufactured there. The stupendous collection of

cf. Plate 70

mosaic pieces once in the hands of Charles V and now in the British Museum and in Florence bears eloquent testimony to late Mexican workmanship in this medium, although most examples were consumed in the *pietre dure* 'laboratories' of Florence in the early nineteenth century.

Highland Mexican artistry radiated to all parts of Mesoamerica in the Post-Classic period, as can be seen, for instance, in the obviously

Plate 75

highland-influenced sculptures and fine perforated and incised shell ornaments from the Huasteca, on the northern Gulf Coast.

Lastly, something might be said of the mentality which enabled the Aztec people not only to survive misfortunes, disasters, and privations which would have broken others, but also to create the most advanced political state ever seen in Mexico. Raised in the most austere fashion, trained to withstand cold and hunger, the Aztec individual embodied ideals which would have done credit to an 'old Roman'. Self-restraint and humility were expected even of those whose fortunes soared.

> *The mature man:*
> *a heart as firm as stone,*
> *a wise countenance,*
> *the owner of a face, a heart,*
> *capable of understanding.*[11]

Not for him the megalomaniac self-esteem and lust for riches exhibited to the Aztec disgust by the Spaniards!

Furthermore, as a curious foil to this optimistic dedication to war, sacrifice, and puritanical ideals there runs a singular streak of melancholy and pessimism in Aztec philosophy, a theme particularly developed by the closely allied Texcocan royal house. The transitoriness of life on this earth and the uncertainty of the hereafter appear in a song ascribed to King Nezahualcóyotl of Texcoco:

> *Even jade is shattered,*
> *Even gold is crushed,*
> *Even quetzal plumes are torn …*

One does not live forever on this earth:
We endure only for an instant![12]

Questions asked in a poem on the same theme:

Will flowers be carried to the Kingdom of Death:
Is it true that we are going, we are going?
Where are we going, ay, where are we going?
Will we be dead there or will we live yet?
Does one exist again?[13]

are answered in another place:

Perhaps we will live a second time?
Thy heart knows:
Just once do we live![14]

THE SPANISH CONQUEST

In the final ten years of the reign of Moctezuma II, strange signs and portents appeared to the terrified monarch. The first of these was a great comet 'like a tongue of fire, like a flame, as if showering the light of the dawn'. Then, in succession, a tower of the Great Temple burned mysteriously; the water of the lake foamed and boiled and flooded the capital; and a woman was heard crying in the night through the streets of Tenochtitlán. Two-headed men were discovered and brought to the ruler, but they vanished as soon as he looked at them. Worst of all, fisher folk snared a bird like a crane, which had a mirror on its forehead; they showed it to Moctezuma in broad daylight, and when he gazed into the mirror, he saw the shining stars. Looking a second time, he saw armed men borne on the backs of deer. Consulting his soothsayers, they could tell him nothing, but Nezahualpilli, King of Texcoco, forecast the destruction of Mexico.

Inflicting great cruelties on his magicians for their inability to forestall the doom which he saw impending, the Aztec monarch was dumbfounded when an uncouth man arrived one day from the Gulf Coast and demanded to be taken into his presence. 'I come,' he announced, 'to advise you that a great mountain has been seen on the waters, moving from one part to the other, without touching the rocks.' Quickly clapping the wretch in jail, he despatched two trusted messengers to the coast to determine if this was so. When they returned they confirmed the story previously told, adding that strange men with white faces and hands and long beards had set off in a boat from 'a house on the water'. Secretly convinced that these were Quetzalcóatl and his companions, he had the sacred livery of the god and food of the land offered to them, which they immediately took back with them to their watery home, thus confirming his surmises. The gods had left some of their own food in the form of sweet-tasting biscuits on the beach; the monarch ordered the holy wafers to be placed in a gilded gourd, covered with rich cloths, and carried by a procession of chanting priests to Tula of the Toltecs, where they were reverently interred in the ruins of Quetzalcóatl's temple.

The 'mountain that moved' was in reality the Spanish ship commanded by Juan de Grijalva, which after skirting the coast of Yucatan made the first Spanish landing on Mexican soil in the year 1518, near modern Veracruz. This reconnaissance was followed up in 1519 by the great armada that embarked from Cuba under the leadership of Hernán Cortés.

From the history of Prescott and in numberless romances many readers are familiar with the stirring events that led to the final death of the Aztec empire at the hands of Cortés. Briefly, the Aztec realm began to fall apart as soon as the conquerors landed, for many of the coastal peoples were only too glad to take the Spanish side against their oppressors. Backed by the advantages of horses, cannons, and huge war dogs, the like of which the Mexicans had never seen, and possessing an incredible fighting spirit, a relatively small band of men marched victoriously up into the highlands. After gaining as their allies the most deadly enemies of the Aztec state, the Tlaxcalans, the Spaniards were allowed by Moctezuma to walk into the great city of Tenochtitlán itself. He welcomed them as gods returning to their own homes and soon permitted himself to be kidnapped by them without resistance in the very heart of the city.

The powerless Moctezuma, alternating between fear and resignation to his own fate, died in the Spanish quarters during the great battle that

Fig. 41

ended with the invaders fleeing the city in the darkness on their way to the coast. It is not certain whether he was killed by Cortés or by the hands of his own people. His place was taken by Cuitláhuac, who reigned only four months, then by the great Cuauhtémoc (1521–24), who directed the fierce Aztec resistance to the returning Spaniards. Realising full well that these foreigners were not gods as Moctezuma had thought, but implacable enemies bent on their total destruction, Cuauhtémoc held off them and their bloodthirsty allies from Tlaxcala, fighting from rooftop to rooftop in the centre of Tenochtitlán, but at a disadvantage against the brigantines which the Spaniards had built on the lake. The last and noblest of the Aztec emperors surrendered his besieged and starving city, its streets reeking with the stench of blood and corpses, on Wednesday, the 13th day of August in 1521. In the true tradition of Renaissance Spain, Cortés received him with honours, only to have him hanged three years later.

Fig. 41. The Old World meets the New, A D 1519. Cortés and friendly nobles of the Tlaxcalan state. From the Lienzo de Tlaxcala

Reigning Monarchs of the Aztec State

Acamapichtli (1367–1387)

Huitzilíhuitl (1391–1415)

Chimalpopoca (1415–1426)

Itzcóatl (1427–1440)

Moctezuma I (1440–1468)

Axayácatl (1469–1481)

Tizoc (1481–1486)

Ahuítzotl (1486–1502)

Moctezuma II (1502–1520)

Cuitláhuac (1520)

Cuauhtémoc (1521–1524)

Text References

With the exception of 6, which is reproduced by kind permission of the publishers, all references are to poems translated by the author from Spanish versions of the original Náhuatl texts.

1 M. León-Portilla, *Los Antiguos Mexicanos a través de sus Crónicas y Cantares*, pp. 21–2. Mexico, 1961.
2 *Op. cit.*, p. 23.
3 *Op. cit.*, pp. 26–7.
4 A. M. Garibay, *Historia de la Literatura Náhuatl*, p. 316. Mexico, 1953.
5 León-Portilla, *op. cit.*, p. 33.
6 Bernal, Díaz del Castillo. *The Discovery and Conquest of Mexico*. Routledge and Kegan Paul, London, 1938.
7 León-Portilla, *op. cit.*, p. 63.
8 Garibay, *op. cit.*, p. 76.
9 Garibay, *op. cit.*, p. 215.
10 Garibay, *op. cit.*
11 León-Portilla, *op. cit.*, p. 147.
12 Garibay, *op. cit.*, p. 103.
13 M. León-Portilla, *Filosofía Náhuatl*, p. 57, Mexico, 1956.
14 León-Portilla, *op. cit.*, p. 218.

Select Bibliography

There has been no attempt to present here anything like an exhaustive coverage of Mexican archaeology, the titles of which run into many thousands. Rather, I have tried to guide the interested reader to those works which might be profitably consulted for further information; many of these publications themselves contain quite extensive bibliographies.

CHAPTER I

The following can be unreservedly recom-
mended as reliable surveys of Mesoamerica as
a whole:

COVARRUBIAS, MIGUEL. *Indian Art of
Mexico and Central America.* New York,
1957.

KIRCHHOFF, PAUL. 'Meso-America', in
Heritage of Conquest, Sol Tax, editor,
17–30. Glencoe, Illinois, 1952.

KRICKEBERG, WALTER. *Altmexikanische
Kulturen.* Berlin, 1956.

MARQUINA, IGNACIO. *Arquitectura Pre-
hispánica.* Mexico, 1951

SANDERS, WILLIAM T., and BARBARA J.
PRICE. *Mesoamerica: the Evolution of a
Civilization.* New York, 1968.

WAUCHOPE, ROBERT, editor. *Handbook of
Middle American Indians.* Austin, Texas,
1975–   (A multi-volume series covering all aspects of life in Mesoamerica.)

WEAVER, MURIEL PORTER. *The Aztecs,
Maya and Their Predecessors.* New York,
1972.

CHAPTER II

AVELEYRA ARROYO de ANDA, LUIS.
'The second mammoth and associated
artifacts at Santa Isabel Iztapan, Mexico',
American Antiquity, xxii, no. 1, 12–28.
Salt Lake City, 1956.

AVELEYRA ARROYO de ANDA, LUIS, and
M. MALDONADO-KOERDELL. 'Association of artifacts with mammoths in the
Valley of Mexico', *American Antiquity,*
xviii, no. 4, 332–40. Salt Lake City,
1953.

DE TERRA, HELMUT, JAVIER ROMERO,
and T. DALE STEWART. *Tepexpan Man.*
New York, 1949.

LORENZO, J. L. 'A fluted point from
Durango, Mexico', *American Antiquity,*
xviii, no. 4, 394–5. Salt Lake City, 1953.

MACNEISH, RICHARD S. 'Preliminary ar-
chaeological investigations in the Sierra de
Tamaulipas, Mexico', *Transactions of the
American Philosophical Society,* xlviii, pt. 6.
Philadelphia, 1958.

WORMINGTON, H. M. *Ancient Man in North
America,* 4th edition. Denver, 1957.

CHAPTER III

BYERS, DOUGLAS S., and RICHARD S.
MACNEISH, general editors. *The Prehistory of the Tehuacán Valley.* Austin,
Texas, 1967–   . (Four volumes have
appeared thus far.)

MacNeish, Richard S. 'Preliminary archaeological investigations in the Sierra de Tamaulipas, Mexico', *loc. cit.*

Mangelsdorf, Paul C. 'Ancestor of corn', *Science,* cxxviii, no. 3335, 1313–19. Washington, 1958.

Mangelsdorf, Paul C., Richard S. MacNeish, and W. C. Gallinat. 'Archaeological evidence on the diffusion and evolution of maize in Northeastern Mexico', *Harvard University, Botanical Museum Leaflets,* xvii, no. 5. Cambridge, 1956.

CHAPTER IV

Coe, Michael D. *The Jaguar's Children: Pre-Classic Central Mexico.* New York, 1965.

Cummings, Byron. 'Cuicuilco and the Archaic Culture of Mexico', *University of Arizona Bulletin,* IV, no. 8. Tucson, 1938.

Dixon, Keith A. 'Ceramics from two Preclassic periods at Chiapa de Corzo, Chiapas, Mexico', *Papers of the New World Archaeological Foundation,* no. 5. Orinda, California, 1959.

Heizer, Robert F., and James A. Bennyhoff. 'Archaeological investigation of Cuicuilco, Valley of Mexico', *Science,* cxxvii, no. 3392, 232–3. Washington, 1958.

Piña Chan, Román. *Las Cultural Preclásicas de la Cuenca de Mexico.* Mexico, 1956.

— *Tlatilco.* 2 vols. Mexico, 1958.

Porter, Muriel N. *Tlatilco and the Pre-Classic Cultures of the New World.* New York, 1953.

— 'Excavations at Chupícuaro, Guanajuato, Mexico', *Transactions of the Ameri-* can *Philosophical Society,* xlvi, pt. 5. Philadelphia, 1956.

Vaillant, George C. 'Excavations at Zacatenco', *Anthropological Papers of the American Museum of Natural History,* xxxii, pt. 1. New York, 1930.

— 'Excavations at El Arbolillo', *Anthropological Papers of the American Museum of Natural History,* xxxv, pt. 2. New York, 1935.

— 'Early cultures of the Valley of Mexico', *Anthropological Papers of the American Museum of Natural History,* xxxv, pt. 2. New York, 1935.

CHAPTER V

Benson, Elizabeth P., editor. *Dumbarton Oaks Conference on the Olmec.* Washington, 1968.

Bernal, Ignacio. *The Olmec World.* Berkeley and Los Angeles, 1967.

Caso, Alfonso. 'Calendario y escritura de las antiguas culturas de Monte Albán', in *Obras Completas,* Miguel Othón de Mendizabal, 6 vols., i, 113–45. Mexico, 1946–47.

Coe, Michael D. 'Cycle 7 monuments in Middle America', *American Anthropologist,* lix, 597–611. Menasha, Wisconsin, 1957.

— *America's First Civilization: Discovering the Olmec.* New York, 1968.

Covarrubias, Miguel. 'El arte "Olmeca" o de La Venta', *Cuadernos Americanos,* v, 153–79. Mexico, 1946.

Drucker, Philip. 'La Venta, Tabasco: a study of Olmec ceramics and art', *Bureau of American Ethnology,* Bulletin 153. Washington, 1952.

Drucker, Philip, Robert F.

Mexico

HEIZER,and ROBERT J. SQUIER. 'Excavations at La Venta, Tabasco, 1955', *Bureau of American Ethnology*, Bulletin 170. Washington, 1959.

JORALEMON, PETER DAVID. 'A study of Olmec iconography', *Dumbarton Oaks Studies in Pre-Columbian Art and Iconography*, 7. Washington, 1971.

STIRLING, MATTHEW W. 'An Initial Series from Tres Zapotes, Vera Cruz, Mexico', *National Geographic Society, Contributed Technical Papers*, i, no. 1. Washington, 1940.

— 'Stone monuments of southern Mexico', *Bureau of American Ethnology*, Bulletin 138. Washington, 1943.

— 'Stone monuments of the Río Chiquito, Veracruz, Mexico, *Bureau of American Ethnology*, Bulletin 157, 1–28. Washington, 1955.

CHAPTER VI
Teotihuacán civilization:

ARMILLAS, PEDRO. 'Teotihuacán, Tula, y los Toltecas', *Runa*, III, 37–70. Buenos Aires, 1950.

LINNÉ, SIGVALD. *Archaeological Researches at Teotihuacán, Mexico*. Stockholm, 1934.

— *Mexican Highland Cultures*. Stockholm, 1942.

MILLER, ARTHUR G. *The Mural Painting of Teotihuacán*. Washington, 1973.

MILLON, RENÉ. *Urbanization at Teotihuacán, Mexico*. Austin, Texas, 1973– . (So far the first two volumes presenting the maps and their interpretation have appeared.)

SEJOURNÉ, LAURETTE. *Un Palacio en la Ciudad de los Dioses, Teotihuacán*. Mexico, 1959.

Cultures of the Gulf Coast:

DRUCKER, PHILIP. 'The Cerro de las Mesas offering of jade and other materials', *Bureau of American Ethnology, Bulletin* 157, 25–68. Washington, 1955.

GARCÍA PAYÓN, JOSÉ. 'El Tajín', *Guía Official, Instituto Nacional de Antropología e Historia*. Mexico, 1957.

MEDELLÍN ZENIL, ALFONSO. *Cerámicas del Totonacapan*. Xalapa, Veracruz, 1960.

PROSKOURIAKOFF, TATIANA. 'Varieties of Classic Central Veracruz sculpture', *Carnegie Institution of Washington, Contributions to American Anthropology and History*, no. 58. Washington, 1954.

STIRLING, MATTHEW W. 'Stone monuments of southern Mexico'. *Bureau of American Ethnology, Bulletin,* 138. Washington, 1943.

Classic Monte Albán:

BERNAL, IGNACIO. 'Monte Albán and the Zapotecs', *Boletín de Estudios Oaxaqueños*, no. 1. Oaxaca, 1958.

CASO, ALFONSO. *Las Estelas Zapotecas*. Mexico, 1928.

CASO, ALFONSO, and IGNACIO BERNAL. *Urnas de Oaxaca*. Mexico, 1952.

LINNÉ, SIGVALD. *Zapotecan Antiquities and the Paulson Collection in the Ethnographical Museum of Sweden*. Stockholm, 1938.

PADDOCK, JOHN, editor. *Ancient Oaxaca*. Stanford, California, 1966.

Western Mexico:

BELL, BETTY, editor. *The Archaeology of West Mexico*. Ajijic, Jalisco, 1974.

SOCIEDAD MEXICANA DE ANTROPOLOGÍA. *El Occidente de Mexico*. Mexico, 1948.

Toscano, Salvador, Paul Kirchoff, and Daniel F. Rubín de la Borbolla. *Arte Precolombino del Occidente de Mexico.* Mexico, 1946.

CHAPTER VII

Acosta, Jorge R. 'Interpretación de algunos de los datos obtenidos en Tula relativos a la época tolteca', *Revista Mexicana de Estudios Antropológicos,* xiv, pt. 2, 75–110. Mexico, 1956–57.

Armillas, Pedro. 'Fortalezas mexicanas', *Cuadernos Americanos,* xli, 143–63. Mexico, 1948.

Burgoa, Fr. Francisco de. *Geográfica Descripcion,* 2 vols. Mexico, 1934. (Contains an account of Mitla.)

Caso, Alfonso. *Interpretation of the Codex Bodley.* Mexico, 1960.

— 'Valor histórico de los códices mixtecos', *Cuadernos Americanos,* lix, 139–47. Mexico, 1960.

Dahlgren de Jordan, Barbro. *La Mixteca, su Cultura e Historia Prehispánicas.* Mexico, 1954.

Diehl, Richard A., and Robert A. Benfer. 'Tollan, the Toltec Capital', *Archaeology,* xxviii, no. 2, 112–24. New York, 1974.

Dutton, Bertha P. 'Tula of the Toltecs', *El Palacio,* lxii, nos. 6–7, 195–251. Sante Fé, 1955.

Jiménez Moreno, Wigberto. 'Síntesis de la historia precolonial del Valle de México', *Revista Mexicana de Estudios Antropológicos,* xiv pt. 1, 219–36. Mexico, 1954–55.

Kelley, J. Charles. 'Settlement patterns in North-Central Mexico', in *Prehistoric Settlement Patterns in the New World,* Gordon R. Willey, editor, 128–39. New York, 1956.

Kirchhoff, Paul. 'Quetzalcóatl, Huemac y el fin de Tula', *Cuadernos Americanos,* lxxxiv, 163–96. Mexico, 1955.

CHAPTER VIII

The literature on the Aztecs is enormous. The really important works on the subject were written either not long after the Conquest, or else in the Colonial period by scholars with access to early records. Of all sources, the monumental encyclopaedia by Sahagún stands supreme, since it is based upon materials written in Náhuatl in the mid-sixteenth century. Regarding the Conquest of Mexico, no account could be more exciting and readable than that of Bernal Díaz del Castillo, who was an eye-witness to the actual events.

The studies by Lewis H. Morgan and his friend Adolph Bandelier on what they held to be a 'democratic' social and military organization among the Aztecs are now thoroughly discredited.

Barlow, R. H. 'The extent of the empire of the Culhua Mexica', *Ibero-Americana,* xxviii. Berkeley and Los Angeles, 1949.

Caso, Alfonso. *The Aztecs, People of the Sun.* Norman, Oklahoma, 1958.

Cortés, Hernán. *The Letters of Cortes to Charles V.* Translated by Francis A. MacNutt. 2 vols. New York and London, 1908.

Díaz del Castillo, Bernal. *The True History of the Conquest of New Spain.* Translated by A. P. Maudslay. London,

1908–16. (American edition, New York, 1958.)

JIMÉNEZ MORENO, WIGBERTO. 'Síntesis de la historia precolonial del Valle de Mexico', *Revista Mexicana de Estudios Antropológicos*, xiv, pt. 1, 219–36. Mexico, 1954–55.

KIRCHHOFF, PAUL. 'Land tenure in ancient Mexico'. *Revista Mexicana de Estudios Antropológicos*, xiv, pt. 1, 351–62. Mexico, 1954–55.

LEÓN-PORTILLA, MIGUEL. *Los Antiguos Mexicanos a través de sus Crónicas y Cantares*. Mexico, 1961.

LINNÉ, SIGVALD. *El Valle y la Ciudad de México en 1550*. Stockholm, 1948.

MONZÓN, ARTURO. *El Calpulli en la Organ-* *izacion Social de los Tenochca*. Mexico, 1949.

SAHAGÚN, FRAY BERNADINO DE. *General History of the Things of New Spain*. Translation from the Náhuatl by Arthur J. O. Anderson and Charles E. Dibble. Sante Fé, 1950–69. (A massive and scholarly encyclopedia of all aspects of Aztec life by one of its greatest students. Book 12 presents an absorbingly interesting account of the Conquest from the native point of view.)

SOUSTELLE, JACQUES. *La Vie Quotidienne des Aztèques*. Paris, 1955.

TOUSSAINT, MANUEL, FEDERICO GÓMEZ DE OROZCO, and JUSTINO FERNÁNDEZ. *Planos de la Ciudad de México*. Mexico, 1938.

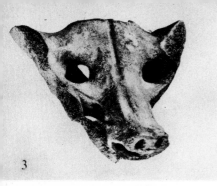

3

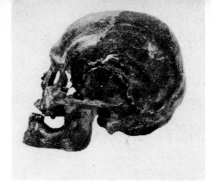

4

5

7

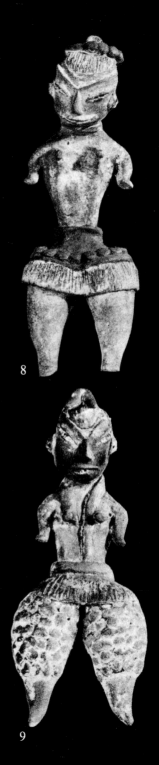

8

9

10

1

14

16

17

18

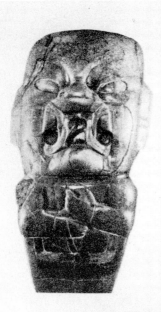

19

20

21

22

4

25

26

29

31

33

34

36

37

38

40

41

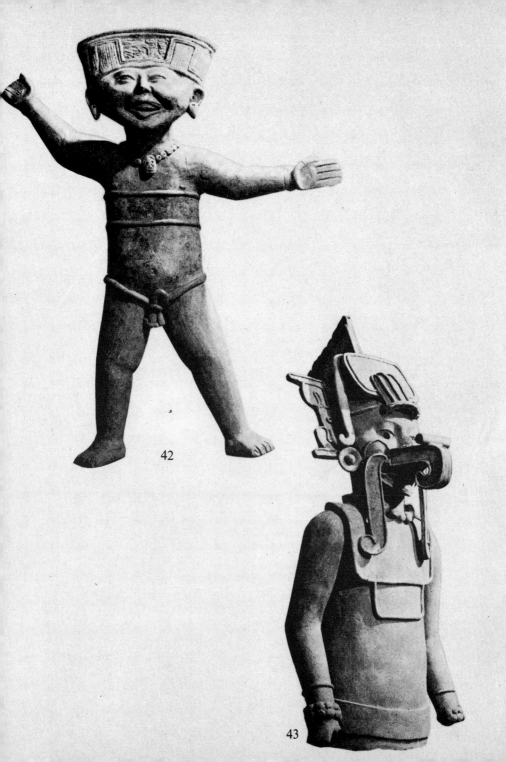

42

43

44

45

46
47

8

49

50

51

53

55

56

57

8

9

60

61

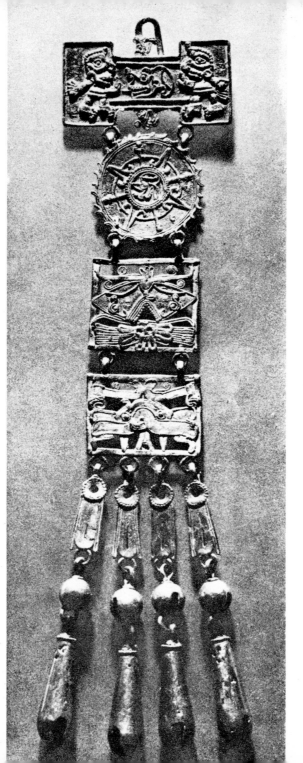

69

70

71

72

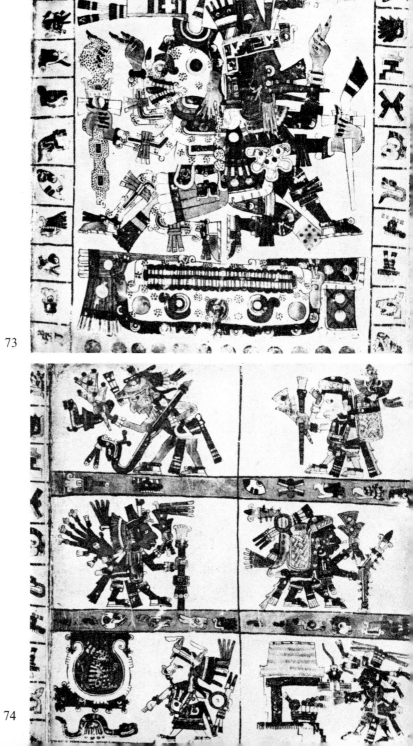

73

74

Notes on the Plates

1 Central highlands of Mexico, near Puebla, with Popocatépetl volcano in the distance.

2 *Chinampas* in the vicinity of Xochimilco, Valley of Mexico.

3 Animal head carved from the sacrum of an extinct llama, from Tequixquiac, state of Hidalgo. Late Pleistocene Age.

4 Fossil human skull from Tepexpan, Valley of Mexico. Late Pleistocene.

5 The second fossil mammoth from Santa Isabel Iztápan, Valley of Mexico, during excavation. The hind leg which had become caught in the mud can be seen in the foreground. During butchering, the head and tusks had been dragged back across the body. Late Pleistocene.

6 View looking northward down the Canyon Diablo from the mouth of La Perra cave, Tamaulipas. From this region and from the Tehuacán Valley has come much of the evidence for the earliest plant domestication in the New World.

7 Pottery figurine of the 'pretty lady' type, Chupícuaro culture. Guanajuato. Late Formative Period. Height about 4 in.

8 Pottery figurine of a dancer, Tlatilco, Valley of Mexico. Height $4\frac{1}{2}$ in. Early Formative Period.

9 Pottery figurine of a dancer, Tlatilco, Valley of Mexico. Height $4\frac{3}{4}$ in. Early Formative Period.

10 Polychrome tripod jar, Chupícuaro culture. Guanajuato. Height $5\frac{1}{2}$ in. Late Formative Period.

11 View west of a portion of the circular temple platform at Cuicuilco, Valley of Mexico. Late Formative Period.

12 Monument 1, San Lorenzo, Veracruz. Height 9 ft 4 in., width 6 ft 6 in. Olmec culture, Early Formative Period. The nearest source of the basalt from which this colossal stone head was carved lies more than 50 air miles to the north.

13 Monument 4, San Lorenzo, Veracruz. Height 5 ft 4 in. Olmec culture, Early Formative Period.

Mexico

14 Monument 2, Potrero Nuevo, Vera-cruz. Two atlantean dwarfs support this basalt 'altar'. Olmec culture, Early Formative Period.

15 North end of Altar 5, La Venta, Tabasco. Over-all height of the monument 5 ft 1 in. Olmec culture, Middle Formative Period. The two adult figures carry were-jaguar babies with cleft heads.

16 Mosaic pavement of serpentine blocks, representing an abstract jaguar mask, one of three known at La Venta. The pavement was cov-ered over with a layer of mottled pink clay and a platform of adobe bricks. Olmec culture, Middle Formative Period.

17 Tomb constructed of basalt pillars, La Venta, Tabasco. The tomb con-tained several burials accompanied by jade offerings and was covered with an earthen mound. Olmec cul-ture, Middle Formative Period.

18 Offering No. 4 at La Venta, a cache of sixteen figurines of jade and serpen-tine and six jade celts, arranged in the form of a scene. Height of figurines varies from $6\frac{5}{16}$ to $7\frac{5}{16}$ in. Olmec culture, Middle Formative Period.

19 Jade effigy axe, known as the 'Kunz' axe. Height 11 in. Olmec culture,

Middle Formative Period, pro-venience unknown. The com-bination of carving, drilling, and incising seen on this piece is charac-teristic of the Olmec style.

20 Small stone figure of a woman and child, provenience unknown. Height $4\frac{1}{2}$ in. Olmec culture, Middle For-mative Period.

21 Wooden mask encrusted with jade, supposedly from a cave in the state of Guerrero. Height $7\frac{1}{2}$ in. Olmec cul-ture, Middle Formative Period.

22 Basalt figure of a bearded man, the so-called 'Wrestler'. Height 2 ft 2 in. Olmec culture, Early or Middle For-mative Period, Arroyo Sonso, Vera-cruz.

23 Bas-relief figure of a 'danzante', Monte Albán, Oaxaca. Monte Albán I culture, Middle to Late Formative Period.

24 Bas-relief figure of a bearded 'dan-zante', Monte Albán, Oaxaca. Monte Albán I culture, Middle to Late Formative Period.

25 Stela 1, Izapa, Chiapas. Height 6 ft 4 in. Izapan style, Late Formative Per-iod. At the top is a band with a stylised mouth representing the sky. Below, a god with reptile-head feet is dipping fish from the water with a

net; he carries a bottle-shaped creel strapped to his back.

26 Fragment of an effigy whistling jar, provenience unknown. Monte Albán I style, Middle to Late Formative Period. The vessel originally consisted of two connected chambers, and when liquid was poured out, air was forced through a whistle in the head.

27 Oblique air-view of Teotihuacán from the north-west. In the lower left is the Pyramid of the Moon. The Pyramid of the Sun lies left centre. The furthest visible group is the Ciudadela, connected to the Pyramid of the Moon by the Avenue of the Dead. The city was laid out on a grid plan, and present-day field boundaries correspond roughly to old foundation walls.

28 Pyramid of the Sun, Teotihuacán, from the west. Height of pyramid slightly more than 200 ft.

29 Giant statue of the Water Goddess, Chalchihuitlícue, from Teotihuacán. Height 10 ft. Early Classic Period.

30 View from the north of the Pyramid of Cholula, Puebla, crowned with a church of the Colonial Period. This great adobe-brick platform, tradi-

tionally dedicated to Quetzalcóatl, rises 181 feet above the surrounding plain and is the most massive structure of the pre-Columbian New World. It was begun in the Formative Period but reached its present dimensions in the Early Classic, under strong Teotihuacán influence.

31 Stone mask in Teotihuacán III style. Life-size. Early Classic Period.

32 Prowling coyote from mural fresco at Atetelco, Teotihuacán. Teotihuacán III culture, Early Classic Period. The painting is done in subtly contrasting values of red. A 'speech scroll' curves from the mouth of the beast, and below the mouth is what is apparently a symbol for the human heart, dripping blood.

33 Stela 6, Cerro de las Mesas, Veracruz. The vertical column on the left records the Long Count date 9.1.12.14.10 (AD 468). To the right, a richly attired figure faces left. His headdress is derived from an Olmec prototype.

34 Carved slate back for a circular mirror, found in southern Querétaro. Diameter 6 in. Classic Veracruz style, Early Classic Period. The reverse side was the reflecting surface, consisting of a consolidated mass of small pyrite crystals.

35 Pyramid of the Niches, El Tajín, Veracruz, looking north-west. Height approximately 60 ft. Late Classic Period.

36 Monument on the steps of Structure 5, El Tajín, Veracruz. The Death God emerges from a complex scroll-work design. Classic Veracruz style, Late Classic Period.

37 Narrow human head of stone, with headdress in the shape of a crane, designed to fit to the front of a stone 'yoke'. Classic Veracruz style, Late Classic Period.

38 *Palma* stone in Classic Veracruz style. Height 20⅛ in. Late Classic Period. The double-strand interlace is highly unusual in this style.

39 Relief panel from the north-east wall of the South Ball Court, El Tajín, Veracruz. The scene depicts the sacrifice of a ball player (the captain of the losing team?). The action takes place in a ball court, and all figures wear the proper paraphernalia: 'yokes', *palmas*, and knee pads. The Death God descends from above to receive the sacrifice. To the left of the scene, the Death God is again repre-sented. Classic Veracruz style, Late Classic Period.

40 Stone 'yoke' in Classic Veracruz style, representing a stylised toad seen

from above, covered with scrollwork patterns. Length about 18 in. Classic Period, possibly beginning of Late Classic.

41 Wheeled pottery toy depicting a deer or a dog, Remojadas style, central Veracruz. The snout and eyes are decorated with asphalt. These amus-ing toys represent the only application of the principle of the wheel in the New World.

42 Pottery figure of a smiling boy, Re-mojadas style, central Veracruz. Height 20½ in. Late Classic Period. The upper teeth of this individual are characteristically filed.

43 Pottery figure of an individual wear-ing the mask of a god, perhaps that of Quetzalcóatl as god of wind. Height 33¾ in. Remojadas style. Late Classic Period.

44 Funerary effigy vessel representing the Rain God, from Cuilapan, Valley of Oaxaca. Height 27 in. Monte Albán III-A culture, Early Classic Period.

45 Building 'M', north-east corner, Monte Albán, Oaxaca. This struc-ture, a platform-pyramid, is of the Monte Albán III culture, Classic Period.

46 Standing figure of stone, Mezcala

style, Guerrero. Height 12⅝ in. Late Formative or Early Classic Period.

47 Stone model of a temple, Mezcala style, Guerrero. Height 4¾ in. Late Formative or Early Classic Period.

48 Pottery house group from Ixtlán del Río, Nayarit. The circular 'floor' has a diameter of 21 in. The chronological placement of this, like almost all western Mexican hand-modelled figures and groups, is unknown but can be no later than the beginning of the Classic Period. Here we see four thatch-roof houses on platforms arranged around a plaza, in the centre of which is a four-tiered, circular temple-pyramid. Among the 50 figures are musicians playing trumpets and rasps, a pair of lovers, water carriers, children, dogs, and five men attempting to seduce a woman. Private collection, Los Angeles.

49 Pottery figure of a man striking a turtle-shell with a deer antler, from Nayarit. Height 14⅞ in. Possibly Early Classic Period. The face and body have been decorated with polychrome paints. Percussion instruments of this sort are still in use in remote villages of Mexico.

50 Seated woman holding a dish, pottery, from Jalisco, western Mexico.

Height 20 in. Probably Proto-Classic Period.

51 Hunchback child, pottery, from Colima, western Mexico. Height 33¾ in. Probably Proto-Classic Period.

52 Oblique air-view of the fortified hilltop town of Xochicalco, Morelos. This site spans the transition between the end of the Late Classic and the Early Post-Classic.

53 View from the south-east of Pyramid 'B' at Tula, Hidalgo. This step-pyramid rises in five tiers and has an over-all height of 33 ft. Toltec culture, Early Post-Classic Period.

54 Colossal atlantean figure of stone, one of the four that surmount Pyramid 'B' at Tula, Hidalgo. Each figure is made of four sections of stone and represents a warrior carrying an *atlatl* in one hand and a bag for copal incense in the other. On the chest is worn the stylised butterfly emblem of the Toltec. Height 15 ft. Toltec culture, Early Post-Classic Period.

55 East side of Pyramid 'B' at Tula, Hidalgo, bas-reliefs of prowling coyotes and felines, alternating with rows of eagles eating hearts and composite monsters. Toltec culture, Early Post-Classic Period.

56 Bas-relief of eagle eating heart, from east side of Pyramid 'B' at Tula, Hidalgo. Toltec culture, Early Post-Classic Period.

57 Stone 'Chac-Mool' from Tula, Hidalgo. Toltec culture, Early Post-Classic Period. Reclining figures of this sort are believed to represent Tlaloc, the Rain God. This 'Chac-Mool' wear the Toltec nose-plug and carries a sacrificial knife strapped to the upper arm.

58 View from the air of La Quemada, a walled hilltop fortress in Zacatecas, north central Mexico. Chalchihuites culture, Early Post-Classic Period. At the right of the picture is the Hall of Columns. La Quemada was one of the most northern outposts of civilisation during Toltec times.

59 The Votive Pyramid, La Quemada, Zacatecas. Chalchihuites culture, Early Post-Classic Period. Contrary to the usual Mesoamerican practice, this was not a platform base for a temple. Instead, the walls originally were continued up to a height of over 30 ft to form the apex of a pyramid.

60 Copper tools and ornaments, Post-Classic Period. The large 'axe-money' is from Mitla, Oaxaca. The awls are from Lake Chapala in Michoacan, the bells and tweezers from unknown proveniences in Mexico.

61 North façade of the Building of the Columns, Mitla, Oaxaca. Over-all height about 26 ft. Early and Late Post-Classic Periods.

62 Portion of inner chamber in Palace II, Mitla, Oaxaca. Early and Late Post-Classic Periods.

63 Gold pendant from Tomb 7, Monte Albán, Oaxaca. Length 8½ in. The pendant was cast by the lost wax process in one piece. The uppermost elements represent, from top to bottom, a ball game played between two gods, the solar disk, a stylised butterfly, and the Earth Monster. Mixtec culture, Late Post-Classic Period.

64 Two carved bones from Tomb 7, Monte Albán, Oaxaca. Length about 7 in. Mixtec culture, Late Post-Classic Period. The representations are calendrical and astronomical in meaning.

65 Façade of Temple I, Malinalco, State of Mexico, a circular temple cut from the living rock. The work was carried out under orders from the Aztec emperors Ahuítzotl and Moctezuma II, between AD 1501 and 1515 (in the Late Post-Classic Period). The outer wall is now about 10 ft high. En-

trance to the interior was gained through a giant serpent face. Within can be seen an outspread eagle in the centre of the floor and above it a feline on a circular banquette.

66 Colossal statue of Coatlícue, the old goddess of the earth and mother of gods and men. Height 8 ft 3 in. The head has been severed from the body, and two serpents rise from the neck, meeting to form a face. Her necklace is fashioned from human hearts and hands, with a pendant skull. The skirt is a web of writhing snakes. Since the goddess feeds on human corpses, her hands and feet are tipped with monstrous claws. Aztec, Late Post-Classic Period.

67 Aztec sculpture reflected in an obsidian mirror with carved wooden frame. Diameter of frame, $10\frac{1}{4}$ in. Aztec, Late Post-Classic Period.

68 Statue of Xochipilli, the Aztec 'Prince of Flowers', patron god of dances, games, and love, and symbol of summertime. Aztec, Late Post-Classic Period. The god sits cross-legged on a temple platform which is adorned with a flower, butterflies, and clusters of four dots signifying the heat of the sun. He wears a mask and is also decorated with stylised flowers and with wild animal skins. Height of figure with base, 4 ft.

69 Carved wooden drum (*huéhuetl*) from Malinalco, State of Mexico. Height $37\frac{3}{4}$ in. Aztec, Late Post-Classic Period. The drum is carved in relief with scenes representing the 'Flowery', or Sacred, War of the Aztecs, symbolised by dancing eagles and jaguars, the sign Four Motion (the present age of the world), and, as seen here in the upper register, the figure of the Sun as an eagle.

70 Sacrificial knife of flint with mosaic-incrusted handle in the form of an Eagle Knight. Length 12 in. Aztec, Late Post-Classic Period.

71 Polychrome pottery cup, from Cholula, Puebla. Mixteca-Puebla culture, Late Post-Classic Period. Height $4\frac{5}{8}$ in. Three jaguars prance around the exterior of the bowl.

72 Page from the Codex Mendocino, a post-Conquest copy of an Aztec original. This is the tribute list of Moctezuma II (1503–20). Pictured on this sheet is the annual tribute due from the six towns of Xilotepec, an Otomí-speaking province north-west of the Valley of Mexico. Enumerated are women's skirts and blouses, men's mantles of various sorts, two warrior's costumes with shields, four wooden cribs filled with maize, beans, and other foodstuffs, and an eagle.

73 Page from the Codex Borgia, now in the Vatican Library. This, the finest of all Mexican manuscripts, was probably painted in Cholula, Puebla. The codex is of deer skin and is folded in screen fashion; it is 34 ft long and 10⅜ in. wide. Mixteca-Puebla culture, Late Post-Classic Period. The scene illustrates the dual aspect of existence, the Death God back-to-back with Quetzalcóatl, the Lord of Life. Around the edge of the page are various days from the 260-day count, one half assigned to the rule of one god and one half to the other.

74 Page from the Codex Borgia. Mixteca-Puebla culture, Late Post-Classic Period. Depicted is the host of the night sky. Represented here, reading from left to right and from top to bottom, are Mixcóatl, the Milky Way; the Traveller of the Southern Sky; Xólotl, the planet Venus; the Traveller of the Northern Sky; the Moon Goddess, before the moon; Tonatiuh, the Sun.

75 The 'Adolescent', sculptured figure from Tamuín, San Luis Potosí. Height 4 ft 4 in. Huaxtec Period V, Post-Classic Period. The body is partly covered with elaborate relief designs which may represent tattoo-ing. On the back, the young man carries an infant in a sling.

Sources of Illustrations

Grateful acknowledgement is made to the following persons and institutions who have kindly provided photographs and permission to publish them:

American Museum of Natural History, New York, 8, 9, 19, 21, 26, 34, 40, 41, 44, 49, 67; Trustees of the British Museum, 70; Compañía Mexicana de Aerofoto, S.A., 27, 52, 58; Robert F. Heizer and the National Geographic Society, 16, 18; Instituto Nacional de Antropología e Historia, Mexico, 3, 5, 7, 22, 31, 59, 63–65, 66, 68, 69, 75; J. J. Klejman, 10; Richard S. MacNeish, 6; Museum of Primitive Art, New York, 20, 38, 42, 43, 46, 47, 50, 51, 71; Peabody Museum of Natural History, Yale University, 60; Arturo Romano, 5; Matthew W. Stirling and the National Geographic Society, 12–15, 17, 25, 33; Hasso von Winning, 48; Yale University Art Gallery and the Olsen Collection, 37; all other photographs are by the author.

Figures 1, 2, 4–6, 8–16, 20–24, 26–40 were drawn by Patrick Gallagher; those based on publications are as follows: Fig. 5: J. L. Lorenzo, 'A fluted point from Durango, Mexico' (fig. 141); Fig. 6: Aveleyra Arroyo de Anda, 'The second mammoth and associated artifacts' (fig. 7), Aveleyra and Maldonado-Koerdell, 'Association of artifacts with mammoths' (fig. 105); Fig. 7: Richard S. MacNeish, *Second Annual Report of the Tehuacán Archaeological–Botanical Project*; Fig. 14: K. Dixon, *Ceramics from Two Pre-Classic Periods* (from a number of figures); Figs. 15 and 16: compiled from M. N. Porter, *Tlatilco and the Pre-Classic Cultures of the New World* and from R. Piña Chan, *Tlatilco*; Figs. 20 and 21: A. Caso, 'Calendario y escritura'; Fig. 23: H. von Winning, 'Representations of temple buildings as decorative patterns on Teotihuacán pottery and figurines' (fig. 1); Fig. 24: A. Villagra, 'Teotihuacán, sus pinturas murales' (fig. 1); Fig. 26: L. Sejourné, *Un Palacio en la Ciudad de los Dioses* (fig. 2); Figs. 27–29: compiled from S. Linné, *Archaeological Researches* and *Mexican Highland Cultures*; Fig. 30: J. García Payon, 'Una "palma" in situ' (fig. 1); Fig. 31: A. Caso, *Exploraciones en Oaxaca, Quinta y Sexta Temporadas* (pl. 1); Fig. 33: J. Acosta, 'Exploraciones arqueológicas en Tula, Hgo.' (fig. 3); Fig. 34: S. Linné, *Archaeological Researches* (figs. 62, 73, 112); Fig. 35: E. Seler, *Gesammelte Abhandlungen*; Fig. 36: *Codex Nuttall*; Fig. 37: R. H. Barlow, *Extent of the Empire of the Culhua Mexica*; Fig. 39: W. Krickeberg, *Altmexikanische Kulturen* (p. 146). Figure 17 is reproduced from a drawing held by the Instituto Nacional de Antropología e Historia; Fig. 25 is reproduced from S. Linné, *Archaeological Researches*; and Fig. 41 by courtesy of the American Museum of Natural History.

Index

Index

Index

Index